SPACE ENCOUNTERS III

Inserting Consciousness into Collision(s)

Revised, Abridged Edition

A True Fantasy Adventure by the Earth
through the Quantum-Entangled World

MARGARET A. HARRELL

PRAISE FOR THE SERIES

"Visually I recognize Margaret Harrell all throughout both books, *Space Encounters* I and II. A sense of her Spirit soaring through the nuances of finiteness is also evident. There is the laughter of the spheres, so to say, in all the spaces. Knowing that God provides or IS all the space and/or spaces—whether we know and acknowledge them or not—a sense of timeless Joy comes forth from the gift of so much space. Creative juices lactated from some yet-to-be-named ductless gland or little-known energy center within, rush forth to . . . DO SOMETHING! Or, CREATE SOMETHING!"
—Al Miner, prestigious channel of Lama Sing, author,
From Realms Beyond

"*Space Encounters* is not so much a report of an experience as the thing itself. That experience, to quote the author, is "to break the umbilical cord that connects us to the single experience, of linearity, called Time." The object is not to leave us in fragments, but to connect us to something larger, not to leave us disoriented, but to reorient us to more expansive energies. *Space Encounters* is an experience well worth having."
—George Stade, novelist, the late professor emeritus of
Columbia University

"Everyone knows the world is in a stuck place. *Space Encounters* III analyzes the problem and encourages us to find a way out."
—Virginia Parrott Williams, PhD,
co-author of *Life-Skills* and *Anger Kills*

Originally printed in unabridged limited edition of 500 by Honterus S.R.L., Sibiu 2003
Simultaneous US & Romanian edition
SÆCULUM UNIVERSITY PRESS

Romanian National Library CIP description:
HARRELL, MARGARET A.
  Space Encounters /Margaret A. Harrell. - Sibiu: Sæculum U.P.S., 2003
  3 vol.; 21 cm

Vol. 3. - 2003. - 552 p. - ISBN 973-99499-9-1
821.111-4=135.1

Credits and Appreciation:
Intricacies of publishing: Didi-Ionel Cenuşer, Ph.D.
Loving start and throughout: Rosa Lee and J. Henry Harrell
Cover image: Grant Goodwine, https://www.grantgoodwineartist.com/
Cover and interior design: Deborah Perdue, https://illuminationgraphics.com

ISBN 2023 hard cover: 979-8-9871061-4-3
ISBN 2023 pbk: 979-8-9871061-6-7

A Published in Heaven Series Book

Published in Heaven Books include titles by His Holiness The Dalai Lama, President Jimmy Carter, Thomas Merton, Seamus Heaney, Hunter S. Thompson, Jack Kerouac, Andy Warhol, Allen Ginsberg, Yoko Ono, William S. Burroughs, Edvard Munch, Diane di Prima, Jim Carroll, Amiri Baraka, Gregory Corso, John Updike, Rita Dove, Wendell Berry, David Amram, Douglas Brinkley, BONO, Ron Whitehead, Lawrence Ferlinghetti, and many more.

Published in conjunction with Saeculum University Press of Sibiu Romania and Raleigh NC

For inquiries, signed copies, and speaking requests,
contact marharrell@hotmail.com
https://margaretharrell.com

BONUS

Go here to listen to Ron Whitehead read his poem
introduction live and to click on Jef Crab's audio

annotations of discussion points in the book.

To that time, the 1990s, when at the touch of a finger, energy streamed forth in printout creations. And this, indeed, provided me with countless bundles—seemingly endless supplies and spurts—of energy. I leave in examples of the "signatures" and draw on examples of the "computer PK," or computer rearrangements of text so that from slivers whole thoughts might emerge and the focus shapeshift, as strips and even single letters took center stage.

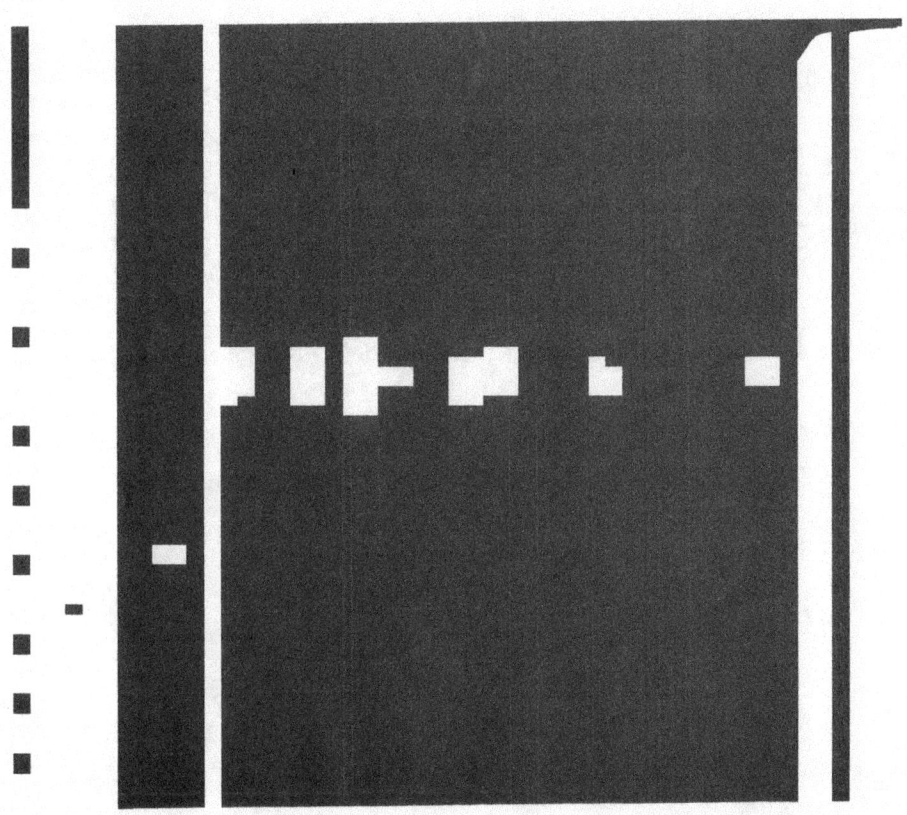

What does this [all] mean? That the essential reality of a system is indescribable? Does it mean that we lack only a piece of the puzzle? Or does it mean, as it seems to me, that we must accept the idea that reality is only interaction?
—Einstein (in *Seven Brief Lessons on Physics*)

CONTENTS

About the Series xi
Introduction by Ron Whitehead xii
Author's Note xv
Preface: Speaking Categorically xix

PART ONE
Chapter One 3
Chapter Two
      Breaking the Container of the Planet 27

PART TWO
Chapter Three
      The Simultaneous Self 37
      And Various and Sundry Uncategorizable Pages
      in Between. 39
Chapter Four
      Reflections on a Theory of Organisms 67
Chapter Four (*cont'd*) 71

PART THREE
Chapter Five
      In Tracing the Vanishing Act 89

PART FOUR
Chapter Six
      Sitting at the Bistro du Dôme 105
Chapter Seven
      So this I am. I am told this upon its arrival. 151

Chapter Eight
     Refuting Ortega y Gasset 197

Chapter Nine
     This time, 2002 205

Caves, Walls, and Begged Questions 221

Creativity: Back to the **Point,** the One-Pointed Focus . . 230

Out of the Stone of Science 251

Cranking Up the End 260
     Romania: In the Cave 262

Not Finished 277

Acknowledgments 285

Afterword by Jef Crab:
Reading Tools and Helpful Insights for Integrating
the Text 286

Dictionary of Multilingual Terms 297

Notes 298

References 300

About the Author 309

ABOUT THE SERIES

*I*nvestigating unconscious strands of connected "Event" bytes, or quanta, the *Space Encounters* series—put together as through the loom of Penelope—follows the voyage of the Earth itself through passages of the past (cast in modern light); at the docking point, some new principles, as well as reminders in biographies of the past, collide.

Slowly, till able to recount the steps—as in a detective story—this ongoing pursuit posits an undeveloped side of chaotic-unfolding, breathtakingly laying it down on the pages as some of the principles operating, till now, unconsciously, throughout the Earth. Inherited (it must be stressed), rather than discovered single-handedly, it is reported, albeit tentatively, inside some mappings of the lives and ideas of famous figures who reveal the workings of this insight.

Margaret A. Harrell thinks of herself more like the custodian of the development of the unfolding ideas in this work; or, on the other hand, Montaigne said: "I am coextensive with what I write."

INTRODUCTION

Discovering the Heart of the World, a Story

All my life I have searched to discover
the path to the heart of the world.

I was determined to discover words
that in some magical mysterious way

might possibly improve on silence.
I abandoned all reason

and wandered the world.
I adventured into and explored unknown lands.

I asked strangers to share their life stories.
With wide open ears

I listened deep and hard
to every word of each story

until I knew them all by heart.
Then I shape shifted the narratives

into poems then
when the evening star opened its eyes

and the crescent moon sighed,
as the great owl blinked,

and the mighty river
flowed over the falls,

on the day before winter solstice,
in a gentle tenor

I softly sang a prayer
to the creative forces of the universe

asking for guidance in finding
the path to the heart of the world.

Then late last night I entered a book,
a book that will be published next year,

a book written by an alchemist of words,
of being. She invited me to read

her newest work. When I opened
the document a wave of electric energy

raced from the tip of my tailbone
to the crown of my head

where it exploded into fireworks.
I shivered and jumped about

in my chair, as if I was having
some kind of spasmed seizure.

Goosebumps all over my body,
I shivered

with excitement.
Then a peaceful calm washed over me.

And I started reading about
quantum energies and creativity.

In no time I saw clearly
that the path to the heart of the world,

a path I had been seeking all my life,
had been with me all along.

Then I understood that
the path is no path at all.

There is no path.
But there is a way, a natural way,

to get to the heart of the world.
The way is to engage

in discourse and collaboration
with other human beings,

with other beings, seen and unseen,
with animals and plants, birds bees trees,

with angels and elemental beings,
with my self, with all and everything.

The path is realized through engagement,
whether solitary or with others.

There is a way of knowing that is beyond
all scientific approaches and methods,

all rational thought. Many are aware of this.
I suspect everyone knows it at some level.

Somehow, everything is unified, one energy,
one never ending spinning whirling.
The ever changing way is discovered
by letting go, listening to the music of life,

of the spheres, then embracing
and enjoying the laughing dance.

Ron Whitehead, Lifetime Beat Poet Laureate

AUTHOR'S NOTE

I catch a glimpse, behind curtains, of three birds outside. Thinking of them, how beautiful they make the world, I push aside the curtain. They fly away.

How did they know, even as (and merely by the fact that) I was there—all three of them? Even before my face was close enough to the glass to see them clearly. Even as I myself was moving the curtain aside. And fly away, even as my hand only brushed the curtain, making no sound in its softness, and yet something—in my focused thought?—communicated TO THEM.

What is this thing called consciousness? Awareness of presence? Communication of presence? How did the birds KNOW?

※

According to a very reliable, firsthand, source, F. David Peat, the physicist and friend of physicist David Bohm, *Bohm had the ability to feel energy dynamics. Here is how Peat described it:*

> Faced with explaining gyroscopic motion, most physics students learn the various formulae, involving conservation of angular momentum, and produce an explanation in a relatively mechanical and formulaic fashion; but Bohm needed *a direct perception of the inner nature of this motion.* Once he was walking in the country, he imagined himself as a gyroscope, and through some form of muscular interiorization, he was able to understand the nature of its motion. In this way he worked out, within his own body, the behaviour of gyroscopes. The formulae and

the mathematics would come later, as a formal way of explaining his insight.

From very early on in his scientific career, Bohm trusted this *interior, intuitive* display as a more reliable way of arriving at solutions. Later, when he met Einstein, he learned that he too experienced subtle, internal muscular sensations that appeared to lie much deeper than ordinary rational and discursive thought.

. . . Bohm himself strongly believed himself part of the universe and that, by giving attention to his own feelings and sensations, he should be able to arrive at a deeper understanding of the nature of the universe.[1] (emphasis added)

"That ability to touch preverbal processes at the muscular, sensory level," Peat observed, "remained with him all his life. It was not so much that Bohm visualized a physical system as that he was able to sense its dynamics within his body: 'I had the feeling that internally I could participate in some movement that was the analogy of the thing you are talking about.'"[2]

Contemporary Taoist Jef Crab concurs:

I am convinced that all new ideas, whatever instigation we receive which means a completely new idea for the collective, coming from somewhere in the stellar, or cosmic, universe, or whatever you want to call it but from a deeper layer of consciousness and information, will always be first noted and absorbed by the physical body through deep muscular changes and impressions, and only afterwards when our deep muscular tissue has a coherent feeling about this, it can transform itself into the brain, into an image, or into an idea. All new information, everything, is first absorbed by the heart, by the deep feeling, the sensitivity, and only afterwards it becomes a thought. Afterwards, when it is evaluated by the heart again, it can become an action. These are abilities the human being has, Heart Center/Feeling, Head Center/Thinking, and the Belly Center/Acting or Willing. All my teachings for the last thirty years are actually focused on people learning to be conscious with this process—exactly what Peat describes here.

PREFACE

Speaking Categorically

*E*verything is energy, traceable back to the fact of atoms. Everything is atoms. Me, you, frogs, trees, stones, books. Everything that is nature, human, chemistry, inorganic chemistry—a fragrance. It is due to the organization of atoms. That means that because these atoms move about and run into each other, colliding, annihilating, changing, being born into a higher or lower energy, they therefore continue carrying the energy of the universe into new situations, new positions, new structures.

If this were not so, there would be no universal order or law, no universe—not the way we know it. These laws are called laws of physics. Where the intersection—the controversy and "problem"—comes in is that certain things seem to violate these laws yet are also composed of atoms. And atoms obey laws. The mind, the soul, the higher mind, the higher realms—could they be beyond the laws of physics?

But the laws of physics, in quantum mechanics, bring us down to the smallest common forms that all life and everything in the universe share. These particles are visible through the motion they instill in what is around them. Visible *by implication*.

Huge accelerators were set up to view the results of subatomic collisions and sometimes catch the energy or move it into specific tasks—all this in tracks the charged particles make.

This book studies us as creatures from the atomic realm (behind that, from Light, the fiery furnace in which the universe, as it first existed as far back as we can trace, emerges)—who therefore, to create more comprehensible human laws, need to know something of energy laws. Because in us and in our cells, governing such basics (sometimes called fatalities) as whether we live or die (whether our cells, unknown to us, have a program, a decision—NOT IRREVERSIBLE—to live or die) are these laws of motion, of conservation; that is, exchanging energy evenly, giving out and replacing so as to have overall stability (what diminishes in one form, in parallel, increases in another). Not that that means *individual* stability.

The balance in the universe subsists inside a system in which things cavort around. One location intensifies when another loses ground. (Alternately, things are at rest but still have energy potentially).

But, as if we were carbon copies, or mere mechanical reminders, of this universal law of conservation, does this *energy exchange of the universe* have to be reflected in human competition?

No. Higher up are laws of love and compassion, justice, mercy, which (qualitative) do not necessarily obey—or not with the same results—these physical laws of conservation of energy (by removing energy from one place if adding in another). On the other hand, they require a kind of detachment, or nonattachment, in application so as to have fields of objectivity.

So these connections—in universal law and the human condition (that is, what it means to be inside physical reality but with the impression that it is NOT MOVING, when in fact, not just in physical objects but in the consciousness always emitted by and born from events, it is)—are some of the preconditions that allow this series to be written. This despite the fact that to describe (observe) might have the effect of removing the energy—thus shifting it to somewhere else.

To hammer that point in, there are the printouts of pages, which illustrate—where common sense and our level of mastery of physical law do not—*that there is some way to override a programmed instruction to the computer.* BY SOME ENERGY LAW.

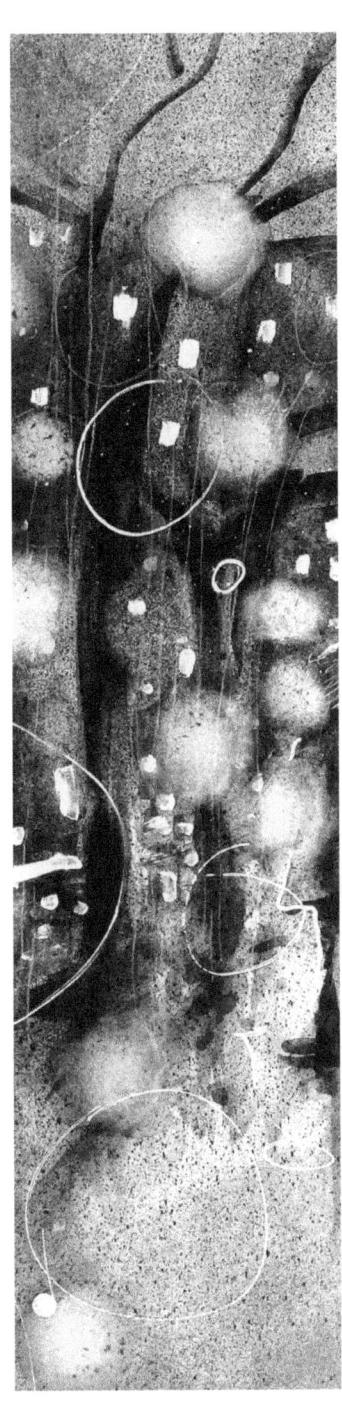

Part One

CHAPTER ONE

*I*n *The Tibetan Book of Living and Dying*, after such chapters as "Bringing the Mind Home," Sogyal Rinpoche begins to talk about the Ground of Dzogchen. "To see directly the absolute state, the Ground of our being, is the View."[3] He quotes Patrul Rinpoche:

> "According to the special tradition of the great masters of the practice lineage, the nature of mind, the face of Rigpa, is introduced upon the very dissolution of conceptual mind." That is, through the dissolution of the "conceptual mind altogether, laying bare the naked Rigpa and revealing explicitly its true nature.
>
> "In that powerful moment, a merging of minds and hearts takes place, and the student has an undeniable experience, or glimpse, of the nature of Rigpa."[4]

※

Now, what I experienced, in a 2001 meditation seminar in which I myself (though not a bird, and supposedly or of course far more complex) received two messages, from two subtle sources whose faces I could see (a message first of all about human beings as *part of the energy system of the Earth*), brought home a pointed message: that through our individual existences, our personal constellations—high up on the complexity scale—humans form an essential *planetary resource*.

As different as we are from oil, wind, solar Light, etc., but just as important, we provide solutions for the Earth—and it is no accident we "manufacture" them.

In the first message I received in that Knokke workshop, I extracted a focus on "having your piece of Earth that you till."

Stepping out of the past of his own life, the speaker, from beyond the "dead," was showing me what information the Earth needs to survive right now, starting—as any such speaker better do—beyond all traditions. You can find this same emphasis inside *The Tibetan Book of Living and Dying*. Let me quote from there, on the value of experience as the East built for centuries on it, discovering ways to verify and to enter even the state of mind where the Mind was Unified:

> What, then, for me is the wonder of Dzogchen [teachings to discover Rigpa, the "Ground" of existence, or the Natural Mind]? All of the teachings lead to enlightenment, but the uniqueness of Dzogchen is that even in the relative dimension of the teachings, the language of Dzogchen never stains the absolute with concepts; it leaves the absolute unspoiled in its naked, dynamic, majestic simplicity, and yet still speaks of it to anyone of an open mind in terms so graphic, so electric, that even before we become enlightened, we are graced with the strongest possible glimpse of the splendor of the awakened state (p. 152).

Everything was obvious, in the experience I myself had of this pristine awareness—obvious by a logic that had not only mental energy but the force of creating the universe.

Staring at the entry moment in the meditation—and then the next—all I could see, as I FELT the sensation of spinning into new depths, all I could grasp, was that each turn "the spinning whole" took, spewing out—refining itself to show—a new facet of The Whole—was self-evident. But I had not known before how to see like this.

Indeed, in reading this text, I realized that surely "a merging of minds and hearts" had taken place, and I had had "an undeniable experience, or glimpse, of the nature of Rigpa."[5] That is what had happened to me. Initially, I was struck dumb in wonder, with no having words or "concepts" to explain or express more than the *sensation* of how meaning appeared, not conceptually—but more by the "logic" of the "obvious."

Now, what does this mean? It is: "I know this. But of course, I know *this too*." Or, as precisely as in a math theorem that is proved, the sensation, the realization, that the only alignment of the second sentence with the first is in a position of: BUT THIS IS OBVIOUSLY TRUE; i.e., the information itself knows; the viewer has only to receive the impact of TRUTH—understanding, at the same time why.

Because there is no other structure possible. It is not that one is suddenly robbed of the ability to argue and build constructs, but that the information, the truths, "build" themselves in some primordial "logic."

Everything was obvious. I knew, and should have known, that for a person whose face had not appeared to me *for seventeen years* (since an initiation in 1985, afterdeath) to suddenly appear in full face, something was up.

Timothy Ferris, who edited *The World Treasury of Physics, Astronomy, and Mathematics*, 1991, pp. 31–32, obligingly gives us these principles:

> The true nature of charge and the reason it comes only in lumps of a certain size are among the most important problems in elementary-particle physics.
>
> The fact that we

fact that w

; been no h

purposes.

at least in

ical forces

ng through

n tube. Al

ications in

The fact that we do not understand charge at a fundamental level
has been no hindrance to making extensive use of charge for practical
purposes . . .

Almost all of the fine control and all of the communications in the world are effected by electrons in electronic circuits . . . If an electric light is plugged in, the electrons are sent flying from one prong of the plug, through the light (where they expend some energy which appears as light and heat), then back to the other prong. The number of electrons involved in such a flow is enormous. In a typical household light bulb, about 10^{19} electrons flow through the filament each second. In heavy machinery or in the high-tension lines connecting cities, the number is far greater. Even through the tiniest and most delicate   electronic circuit, many billions of electrons flow each second.

If a comb is passed through dry hair, perhaps a million million electrons leave the hair and stick on the comb . . . It is fortunate for us that the objects in our macroscopic world remain always almost neutral. If the comb acquired anything close to an electrification of one extra electron per atom, the consequence would be dire. Either there would be a powerful and deadly bolt of lightning from comb to man as the charge was neutralized or the enormous force of electrical attraction would draw the comb back so violently that it would be a dangerous weapon . . .

In every object in our world, the number of positive charges is almost precisely equal to the number of negative charges . . . If a big imbalance were ever realized (there is no chance of this) the disastrous result would make the force of gravity appear to be truly inconsequential."[6] (emphasis added)

The principles were stated here. Charge, with an attraction—as theoretical physicist Kenneth William Ford, put it—like French perfume" (that is, "that certain something worn by particles which makes them attractive—specifically attractive to the opposite kind of particle") is mysteriously balanced in Nature.[7]

As Ford states, "Man has proceeded so far away from the familiar scale of the world encompassed by his senses, that he must make a real effort of the imagination to relate these new frontiers [of science] to the ordinary world. But *the reward of being able to think pictorially over the whole panorama, from infinitesimal to enormous, adequately repays the effort.*"[8] (italics added)

Some of the principles of charge I had been shown in personal experience, as some of it is commonsensically familiar to everyone.

But just look at physicist Carlo Rovelli's conjectures. Rovelli, working at the Center of Theoretical Physics at Aix-Marseille University, is a founder of loop quantum gravity theory: *in quantum gravity, he says, what you deal with is relations, nothing but.*

Forget about individual humans and things, achieving visibility in non-relationship situations. They must relate to get noticed, to get existence. Tell that to everyone, shout it from the rooftops. We are all, even if not by choice, part of something, down on this level. Loop Quantum Gravity (LQP) theorizes—because most of the understanding about us on this level is at the theory stage—that space and time take the form of—you guessed it—loops, aka spin networks.

In fact, in today's speculations, it is not even clear that cause and effect are the correct sequence. What about if cause-effect/effect-cause are given equal weight because of something called "superposition"? More on that later. *But you are not going to tell me that the effect I see with my very own eyes could theoretically be the cause? Yes, that is the finding.* "Physicists have long sensed that the usual picture of events unfolding as a sequence of causes and effects doesn't capture the fundamental nature of things. They say this causal perspective probably has to go if we're ever to figure out the quantum origin of gravity, space and time."[9]

At the Tate Gallery in London Rovelli visited Cornelia Parker's exhibit *Cold Dark Matter*, consisting of large-scale installations of scattered reconceived everyday objects. Rovelli says it "mirrors his take on the nature of reality."

Most famously in 1991 she persuaded the British army to blow up a garden shed stuffed with everyday clutter before suspending its blasted fragments, constellation-like, around a single lightbulb under the title *Cold Dark Matter: An Exploded View*. A creative reflection on the Big Bang Theory, the work was also made

> at the time of the IRA bombings in the UK. It is now one of the most popular works in Tate's collection and features prominently in Parker's major retrospective at Tate Britain . . . She was keen to stress that the elaborate negotiations, conversations and processes she engages in while making her multifarious oeuvre are as much a part of the work as the end product.

That is, "I connect with the process: of her coming up with the idea, producing the idea, telling us about the idea and of us reacting to it . . .," Rovelli says. "We don't understand Cornelia Parker's work just by looking at it, and we don't understand reality just by looking at objects." In fact, in his relational quantum mechanics, "objects don't exist in their own right." He wants us to "rethink reality in terms of relations, instead of objects, entities or substances."[10]

Marking reality—Marking Time—is that what it's all about— as I intuited in writing about Faulkner? Just like the particles, we bang into——run into, stumble upon—each other?

Whether commonsensical or mind boggling, the laws of a whole new frontier of science pervasively work in the *subparticle level of all energy*. Matched to what I had been shown, these laws made unknown laws that apply to us perceivable. For my small part, it was no "flash" exactly, but to have been in the right place, to have registered when the right information came.

To quote myself:

> As many scrambled to articulate more clearly these laws of gravity, at least as it applied in the microworld and to machines and technology, the real low-down will perhaps turn out to be that and something else

entirely. How do I know? Well, because I was shown, but didn't know how to get the message across. Till sudden ly, now, recently, I *encountered*

tirely. How do I know?
  didn't know how to get the
y, now, recently, I *encountered*

a mind, traveling through mental space, and it focused me here. And said: NOW, *go ahead. Explain. Tell the Earth this law,* SO IT CAN USE THIS ONE and go on to others, . . .

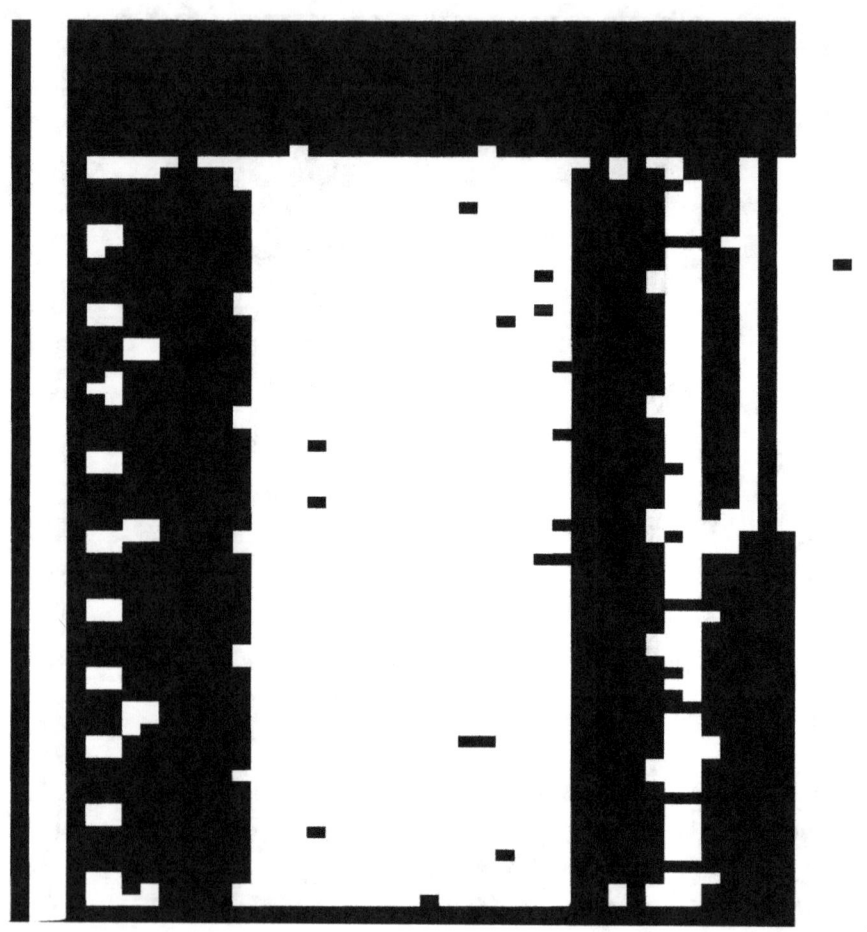

But first, this one is urgent. The earth has NEED OF IT in order not to make unnecessary mistakes in using its technology as if it had no repercussions, unneeding of warning, as if a playtoy. Or as if it were a tool like fire. And we all know—SUPPOSING IT IS—fire burns.

My meditations in a Knokke, Belgium, seminar in March 2001 began to draw in the long rope I was out on, focusing me back and back toward right here, with all I had set out to say, bring in, even from the stimulation point of view—but also from hard experience—to the twenty-first century thought experiments, art investigation, and just plain guinea-pig reports.

The disclosures, the bolt of lightning, that came out of that were so startling and timely (urgent, synthetic) that I describe the situation here in more detail—the revelation being something I will never forget, captured in a kernel of language:

Far from a sense of ineptitude and helplessness before problems we face, it had spoken to me entirely of solutions. Where were they?

INSIDE HUMANS.

Simply put, problems paralleled the possibility of solving them!! To find the solutions, we *prospected ourselves*! And an equation existed to that effect.

No problem came into being without its solution, there in our deep human *mines*, in the grappling with it of some one or several of us, some "coal or gold or diamond mind" just waiting to deduce it. We had it covered, in the problem/solution equilibrium—symmetry—inside us.

More, the potential solution power we humans had—were dynamically composed of in "raw" information (which was as complex as the many potential combinations of individuals)—if truly mined and explored, was (even mathematically) roughly proportional to the number of *problems*.

Learning the secret equation, I felt as if hit with a thunderbolt. Exploring dormant human potential was *mandated*. Our solutions, waiting out the scene, the "act" of the play, depended for activation on individual human processing. That is, humans getting out shovels and spades and lawnmowers and clippers and in all ways staking out their claims, beautifying their potential within. *Here, in our energy, located inside the memory banks and experiential reasonings and answers dormant in individuals and the collective, was the hope of tomorrow. Buried, waiting* CREATION. *In the creative energies themselves!!*

No longer could exploration be *outside only*. In 2001 this stunning news, entering my mind in the Knokke light body seminar meditation, was stated outright. Digging into "our own piece of Earth, *each of us* had cradles of solutions the planet needed. What was outside us collectively, in a problem, coexisted with a *correlating* inner solution potential. Each of us was as essential as the planetary resources of oil or uranium or solar energy or water, wind, metals, or anything else—if not more so. A secret resource the Earth counted on to hold its information capacity. But we had better—

GET STARTED.

The Guardians of the Earth held a council.

The second "message" I received at the March 2001 seminar identified a different collective issue, again from the point of view of the Universal Mind. In this meditation I found myself in a "council meeting"; there, the topic was the impact of planetary change on karma ("lessons," or "debt," that, from one point of view can be translated into "opportunity" but doesn't always play out that way); the workings of karma, they observed, was too dangerously flawed—had a loophole which unintended consequences could easily fall in.

In times of massive change, a person vulnerable through the smallest of lessons (a fragment not totally learned, a residue of a repeated mistake, a momentary wanning in insight) might fall, struck by the very same weight as someone who truly needed the lesson (long overdue).

Receiving this insight from the Lord Vishnu consciousness through the powerful presence, including face, of Dhyanyogi Madhusudandasji (Guruji), also having "dropped the body," I had to accept—and did—the hypothesis that intelligence itself was more advanced in some "places" than here in what is generally known as the Earth consciousness; that in some fashion what might be called "advanced intelligence" watched over the development of the Earth and faced such questions as when to interfere (if to interfere).

What constituted "interference," and what "protection"? Should the Earth merely be left alone as these uneven workings of karma occurred in massive planetary upheaval? No, if the Earth was to go through a Transition, something must be done."

That is, if the Earth were speeded up, in what it had—for some good reason, unknown to us—to integrate. To reread, to pass before its eyes as questions, just as if in an encounter with the Light. Or, as if the energy of the Earth was having these challenges and the tables were turned: the collective level was on one speed (in the consciousness), where events were raced through, while—on the "everyday" level, where people lived—everything went much slower, each event involved whole lives, sometimes definitively affected the people encountering them.

But what does that mean—"go through a transition"? I had immediately picked up on the terms, as if expecting it, in hearing the announcement

"NO TRANSITION . . . Debauchery"

Starting THERE, I established the title for the LOVE *in Transition* series, which preceded *Space Encounters*.

Years later, it was THE WHOLE EARTH—announced, to those who were paying attention, as being

ITSELF

IN TRANSITION.

CHAPTER TWO

Breaking the Container of the Planet

So, at the beginning point of another expansion quantum gravity is conceived of as laws *of relationship: dynamic interaction*. And different unit-sizes—event chunks, time chunks.

> When you read a message on a piece of paper, your brain becomes correlated with it through the photons that reach your eye!!!!! [emphasis added] Only from that moment on will you be capable of remembering what the message said. As Lloyd put it, "The present can be defined by the process of becoming correlated with our surroundings."[11]

What this means: I *merge with my surroundings*.

The new revelations fed back into my own experience, REGISTERED 100 percent on the Richter scale of what I could imagine was true.

I had this idea handed to me. Not without a lot of work. And that will bring in THE NEXT LAW.

"It has to be recognized that every measurement is really the statement of a ratio." (p. 36, Ford in Ferris, ed.)

That mass is one of the forms of

energy was first realized at the beginning of [the twentieth] century. The energy of mass and the energy of motion are the two forms of energy which dominate the elementary-particle world. Mass energy can be thought of as the "energy of being," matter possessing energy just by virtue of existing. A material particle is nothing more than a highly concentrated and localized bundle of energy. The amount of concentrated energy for a motionless particle is proportional to its mass. If the particle is moving it has still more energy, its kinetic energy. A massless particle such as a photon has only energy of motion (kinetic energy) and no energy of being (mass).

Einstein's most famous equation, $E = mc^2$, provides the relation between the mass, m, of a particle and its intrinsic energy [latent, locked-in, unused, being withheld], or energy of being, E." (pp. 27–28)

"Surprisingly enough, in Einstein's first paper he did not use E for E*nergie* or Energia in German and Greek respectively, c for *celeritas* (swift in Latin), but rather L for energy . . . and V for the velocity of light" (p. 29, Peter Galison, "The Sextant Equation: $E = mc^2$," in Farmelo, ed.).

The point being that to a form to which movement was definingly central—modeled more along the lines of light—then not to move would deactivate the sensory or frequency system. The frequency would fall, slow down, not be able to detect "change" or "difference" as at higher speeds. Acquire what seemed, or in fact was, the state of death relative to what to it expressed the only meaning of life—which was to move. Inside the spectrum of electromagnetism, of light, etc., and of any of the "forces," it goes without saying that there will be movement. But why is consciousness left out of this grouping? Does not consciousness too (inside each person) need the new picture of itself as SOMETHING THAT MOVES???

p. 24:

The new particles, or "resonances," now being discovered have lifetimes of 10^{-20} sec. or less . . . They are like the car which collapses before it gets out of the factory gate. The manufacturer might be tempted to say, "That was no car; it was just an unstable phenomenon with a transitory existence" (for which the physicist uses the word "resonance").

But we stop here. FINALLY. We pick up EXACTLY HERE, in a

nnouncing a principle I hold dear, but that caused me great embarrassment in first learning it, in 1985 in my Zurich Initiation. I believed everything I was told in the initiation, which well I should have, as it was true—true if you focus on your cosmic energy and location(s)—but was well beyond my capacity to integrate it, so I received it mechanically, *looking superstitious.* You can imagine how that worked—how awkward I seemed—when you read the next pages, with me in the dark, trying to apply this law in a world where at every second we are touching something. *But touch! How could I allow that! Just think of the chains of meaning I had just been apprised of—how that worked.* So, I was unaccountably and undeniably odd in this period if I dared go out. Dared I? I wrapped myself in knots. You decide.

�֎

A thing is never just a thing in itself, irrefutably standing alone in the world, arriving here bereft of its past, its surroundings, the "memory" the universe has embedded it in. Where it has been— be it an everyday table fork not carefully washed, a shoe walked in from the fields, a leaf the hand touched—carries the trace energy, or memory traces (latent but still there), of the *chain,* the presence, *of what it connected to before.* Lordy, but we are always touching things. It's an identifying sense we have. We love to do it, heedless of the history of the object. And yet—I had it explained to me by a cosmic guide—these objects we unthinkingly touch have tiny "memories" that mean the object carries with it the tendency of continuing on in the same sequence, reproducing it, falling even into the *sequence* again!! Like DNA chains, these "touch chains" carry—a history.

Yes, like the lingering impression the just-closed eye momentarily holds onto of the last image seen—carries into the dark—these prior impressions stick to touch as well.

At first blush one would say the implications are radical. However, I assure you now, this procedure is not mechanical. It *can be countered.* Or be too faint to matter.

Regardless, this level of subtle influence surrounds us—

implying a *sense of the invisible path*, just as the grooves in our brain carry imprints, memory traces, tendencies, communication based on them. Apparently obvious, this leads to more and more subtle implications.

When I first learned this, novice that I was, I became hypersensitive to whatever I touched, afraid of such a tiny thing as a fork; overreacting superstitiously *as if I had no authority, no consciousness, to counteract the chain influences.* But that was ridiculous—I did, of course—but I responded with a shock at glimpsing yet one more energy law we do not know (I certainly didn't). However, I assure you I have come a long way since then, since 1985 and my blockbuster initiation, first becoming personally aware of our position in the universe of unknown laws, unknown secret (to us) workings.

More later, to back this up.

It is as if gravity is not just the easiest (previously used) pathway around a mass, *which causes that path to exist*, so that everything, from bending sound waves to circling planets, is affected by the presence of the mass, altering course to accommodate. But is itself MULTIDIMENSIONAL; i.e., involving not only form (or travel lines based on geodesics) but radiations that exist in reference *to its content*, even if this is explained not by consciousness existing in the locations (locally), but resonance itself! This, however, relying on relativity of speed, because if on a speed too different, the resonance is not apparent. Nothing lines up. There is DIS-CONNECT.

Part Two

CHAPTER THREE

The Simultaneous Self

*I*s it possible?

What is it?

And Various and Sundry Uncategorizable Pages in Between

If these probabilities were always changing, which meant the mind's grasp of the whole content in them was changing, then there was no shock *to the mind*, to realize that it could meet the potential of the future in a way that directly influenced what that future was. Fully take responsibility for the implications of present action, extended beyond what effect it could be thought to have. But it could learn to think that far "in a second." To bring the future up; say, *How shall we work on it now*? BEFORE IT HAPPENS. That each decision taken now either continues in this direction OR SHIFTS. Even—through the laws of motion—begins an entirely different sequence, sets into motion an entirely different course of events.

To further complicate the picture, another experience—that doesn't fit Earth description of reality—has happened repeatedly to me, for years: I lie in bed, almost asleep. Suddenly, distinctly, the energy shifts to a high level. I recognize that I am in "tomorrow." Yes, somehow I got there. The energy exists there and I'm in contact with it. I've been taken to it or it's come to me. It's my energy *in the future*. In a specific scene, a time and place then. Here. Now. I know that it's presenting a bit of an experience from tomorrow to me. How?

Why is easy—so I'll be energetically prepared to go into it on a high vibration. To me, it has always happened through a spirit guide. Even if one part of me didn't believe in spirit guides, another part of me explained to me that this was the explanation. I was being shown this moment in the future, energized as if showered with white electric light, making me experience it on that level beforehand. Then when this principle, this moment, operative in my bedroom, withdraws, I can confidently expect that, as in rehearsing for an exam in university, I am all prepared for the future moment, the next day, as I have run through it in very subtle, high energy. My experience of it is all set up. It cannot fail.

It rests on the fact that if time is not linear, I can experience this segment of "tomorrow" today; in this case, the night before. Future before past. This calls on a reality fixture we do not believe in. But it comes to us. To me. By it, I know that I am not entirely three-dimensional. It lives in my life, as if I believed in the principle. And I do. I have to. What a shift, if I can live bits of my life out of sequence.

If I resisted—in this type of case I never did—the information might be precipitated by dreams followed by a tension headache as if the skull had to be loosened with a wrench, as if there had to be more space made. As if a skullcap had come to sit there—being merely the recognition of this state—that felt that way not relative to oneself the day before, but relative to this new energy that or who or which made one feel how different one was from it—at odds—if one didn't want to go in the new direction, which was to see into the future. The future that this course led into, which already existed—like a territory—at the end of this.

bC

Newton had already said that attraction increased or decreased in intensities and force. It did this relative to distances and mass.

This topic introduced, we will start here. To take the formula and transcribe it, in energy terms, into its implications, now that we can see better what energy is, these many years hence See more how, quite normally, these attractions work in our lives. That we take for granted, without noticing the obvious, or not being too concerned about it: that they are laws with *implications* extending into where we can no longer see. And thus lose all vocabulary—except incredulity, etc.

In the case of a huge point being made, one has no choice but to finish one's life, even, without going ahead on one's independent personally critical trajectory but to join in the slower, and lagging, one—of the world's. One has seen this, many times before, where someone makes a leap and the entire earth wants to follow. But not at the same pace as the initiating one. Again, the fact being that there are other entities and shapes and forms and speeds than that of Alpha-Omega. One lags rather than races, toward the finishing of the beginning. Thus, I was beginning (yes, with many lags to the understanding, many embellishments, paintings, interior assessments, and detours) to go toward the CONCLUSION OF THIS ONE THOUGHT, how it evaluated its own self, relative to the possibility of there being things inside itself it LEFT OUT.

Obviously, this had been known long before.

But I *hadn't known it. Had been spared this knowledge.* Had almost had a "blind spot."

For my own protection, as is always true, in some degree. Here, in large measure, perhaps. Take Einstein's admiration of Newton, partly for the very reason that he dared to be wrong. On a point. And for this, Einstein greatly admired his ability to pick out the essential, given the time limits, so as to give something useful to the age, however limited a detail or two were. Therefore, he apologized to Newton in proving him wrong: "Enough of this, Newton, forgive me; you found the only way which, in your age, was just about possible for a man of highest thought—and creative power" (p. 589, "Autobiographical Notes," in Ferris, ed.).

However, we will definitely avoid taking any mystery from the Earth, only shifting a few locations.

We will not be AT A LOSS—as formerly. There was not then the capacity to put into words "Time Entrapment." Trapping us like mice, etc. If we let it. So, we start here. Or stop here. To be picked up Further ON.

※

A Provocative Excerpt from Timothy Ferris's *The Whole Shebang*:

> We humans, having come along when the universe was already billions of years old and being rather *big* creatures, able to see stars in the

sky but not atoms in an apple, naturally got into cosmology from the large-scale side of things—by observing galaxies and developing theories, such as relativity, to interpret their behavior. But the universe was not always big and classical. Once it was small and quantum, and possibly it has not lost the memory of those times. It may well turn out that over there—or, more properly, inside and underfoot, marbled through the very fabric of the space that is in turn marbled through every material object—the universe remains as it was in the beginning, when all places were one place, all times one time, and all things the same thing.

After introducing John Stewart Bell's demonstration that nature does not work in a local—mechanistic—way, but that two particles that start out together, when later separated, then if one is observed, the other instantly reflects knowledge of that, he goes on to describe *nonlocality* and states that physicist Henry Stapp called Bell's theorem "the most profound discovery in science:

> We encountered the concept of *locality* earlier in this chapter, as the supposition that one system can change another only if there is some sort of mechanical interaction between the two . . . To say that fiddling with one particle over here can *instantly* influence its sister particle over there is to assert that subatomic particles behave in a *nonlocal* way. This would overthrow the time-honored assumption of locality, and that is what Einstein found so repugnant about the situation, and why he constructed the EPR thought experiment to highlight its apparent irrationality.

Bell—a red-bearded experimentalist who spoke with a soft, Northern Irish burr, and whose unassuming wit concealed an exceptional tenacity of mind—pondered this matter for years, focusing on its essential question of whether natural processes obey locality, as had traditionally been thought, or are in some way nonlocal on the quantum level. In a paper published in 1964, he proposed an experiment that could finally settle the matter . . . They involved testing the polarization of large numbers of photons. Their significance was that they would produce different results if the particles behaved in a local way, as Einstein insisted, or in a nonlocal way, as the quantum mechanics equations mandate. This distinction is, after all, what all the bother over quantum weirdness is about. In both cases, and in all experiments conducted since, the verdict is clear. [Niels] Bohr was right (nonlocal effects do occur in quantum systems) . . . Nature—on the subatomic scale at least—really is nonlocal. Fiddling with one particle really does mean that its sister particle is altered, instantly, even if it is far away, and neither hidden variables nor any other mechanistic scheme can rescue Einstein's belief in locality. As the physicist F. David Peat puts it, "The choice before us is either to abandon any hope of knowing the nature of quantum reality or to accept a nonlocal universe." . . .

So, let's look at the alternative—"to accept," in Peat's words, "a nonlocal universe."

What might that mean? It *might* mean that the universe is interconnected in some deep and as yet only dimly perceived way, on a level where time and space don't count . . . A capable etymologist [in *Wholeness and the Implicate Order*].

Bohm used the word "implicate" in its sense of "enfolded." He suggested that nonlocal effects are woven through the universe in something like the way that a chef folds cream into a sauce. For Bohm, classical physics dealt with an *explicate* order, the mechanical world of Newton's gravity and Einstein's relativity, while quantum mechanics was the first science to examine the implicate world of nonlocalities. A scientific clue to this vision may be found in the odd consideration that photons do not "experience" time . . . At light speed, the speed that photons move in a vacuum, there is no time at all. So a photon "traveling" from point A to point B does so, from its point of view, in zero time—meaning that, in some sense, the two points aren't separate! Another clue comes from the work of John Wheeler and others on the hypothesis that space is interconnected by multitudes of wormholes, little tunnels linking localities that to us seem far apart . . .

Bohm and others have likened the implicate universe to a hologram (from the Greek, "to write the whole") . . . Shatter a hologram, put one of its fragments in the laser beam, and what you see is not a piece of the original image but *all* of it. The image is dimmer and a bit 'noisier,' but spatially the whole thing is there, in this and every other fragment.

What if the universe is like that? I don't know how to frame such a concept in contemporary scientific terms, so I won't try. Such difficulties may, of course, be a signal that there *is* no "'implicate" side to the universe—that this line of thought is just hot air. But they also might mean that, as Bohm believed, we are indeed dealing with a new "order," which must therefore evolve its own concepts and language and cannot properly be analyzed, in Bohm's words, "to make it fit well-defined and preconceived notions as to what this order should be able to achieve." So let me describe the concept more generally, as a kind of fable. (pp. 283–287, Ferris, *The Whole Shebang*)

An interesting law (interesting if one jumps with delight at the proximity of something challenging, the injunction to keep going) is that when I read a book, if I could reference myself relative to that book, I could find out what I think about the subject before reading what the author says. This, of course, is supposed to be impossible: to speak to that me. It is another finding so important it bears underscoring at the start. But it is not just dependent on speaking to "that me," which might perhaps tentatively be labeled "going into the future." That is, extending one's present self into the *implied self*, who had the ability to acquire this information. But did not

1L

EXIST. We can imagine descriptions of time, to be explored later on, in which this self did exist (perhaps like one of the dimensions, in string theory, that is said to be "curled up," therefore small and inaccessible, and not part of the standard known dimensions, three plus time). Implied in the fact that I would read this book and acquire this information. For instance. So: if I could talk to this self, by stepping out into the RIM where that self existed and had thoughts about the subject, I could

REFERENCE MYSELF.

It would greatly expand Information Theory.

Going at least as far out, Jef Crab, founder of the E.A.S.T. (Energetic Awareness Sensitivity and Transformation) Institute, illuminatingly recalls:

> Now, during my life I experienced many times that even by reading fragments of a theory, scientific or not, I could in some way put a complete image of this theorem in my head. I observed this already very early in middle school. I saw that fragments of information were enough to clarify a lot of things to me. Later on, in the [Belgian] secret service, or special forces, I noticed that with codes and so on I could do the same thing. Later still, I started realizing that there was a difference between an analytic thinker and a synthetic thinker; analytic thinkers actually analyze their observations and then they try to connect the dots. With a synthetic thinker, instead of first of all taking all the parts of a puzzle, it's like starting from one point—from this induction—seeing the relevant pieces of the puzzle surrounding it.
>
> Even later, I started to understand, from Taijquan—the Chinese philosophy—that in fact things are synchronistic, holistic, and that even with fragments of information we are able to put together a whole theory, which is why some years ago I stopped reading books. I satisfied myself with just bits and pieces, which came to me by whatever means they came to me, and noticed that I just started evolving the whole theory in my head. All my ideas about society and ethical ecology, the E.A.S.T. theory, etc., they came out of the same source of

information. And what I am trying to describe is a certain state of mind—a state of being—in which we become holistic instead of analytic.

✵

Truth be told, quite by accident while living in Zurich in the 1980s, I discovered I could be in one room and "access" the *topography* of my manuscript from another room—that is, assess, mentally, the energy "shape": the contours of "mountains," "hills and valleys," or dead spots—which I then used to make revisions upon sitting in front of the physical-manuscript later in the day. Or next day. I had primed myself unconsciously, and that knowledge popped easily into consciousness when I sat down again at the typewriter (yes, no computer yet).

As this progressed, I discovered the same ability after I moved to Belgium. It worked from my Tai Chi class, taught by Jef in Leuven—fifteen minutes by train from Tienen, where the physical manuscript lay. In moving my hands through the air in the Tai Chi forms, I could work in the manuscript "topography," aware of the energy "shape," the "geography," though not the words, priming myself for going through word revisions consciously, quickly, back at home in front of the text.

But is this not operating under the principle by which Einstein overturned the old law of gravity (as a mysterious "attraction at a distance"), substituting that erudite General Theory of Relativity, whereby it was warps and shape changes in four-dimensional "space-time" caused by mass that created what mascaraded as gravity? Because he refused to call it gravity. No, it was mass exerting the "pull." And wasn't that what I was sensing by feeling, the "mass" represented by this "topography"? He did not call it gravity, as said. Not that everyone at all agreed. No, this set off a firestorm of disagreement.

Back to Socrates, who wished information in a book could converse with the reader. A wish perhaps based in this knowledge, forgotten yet speaking in its oblique reference to itself. Thus, if Socrates "remembered" it was possible to talk to a book, sitting it in the room and drawing forth its comments in interactive dialogue and without even necessarily knowing that one did this, the motivation for the depth of feeling behind his comment was that he knew this principle. Deep within, it stated itself as a "quarrel," a dissatisfaction, with the way things were.

Now, this is around 2,400 years later,* and the "sleeping prophet" Edgar Cayce, for one, notoriously reported experiencing reading a book while asleep, in close proximity to it. And definitely my mind, in editing, "goes ahead" to insert words that I have to minutes later then retract because I find them just a few paragraphs further down the page; I imagine this is because, as Max Planck, in giving the name "quanta" to quantum physics, discovered, "lumps" of energy have *a fixed relationship to their frequency*. My proximity to the frequencies, then, allows them to "speak" to me if I pay attention.

After much struggle, the idea makes its own way into *its* future, landing right at quantum physics' door, as if Plato himself said: W*ait!* I *have something to say here*. (I hope the reader gets the intended humor.) I needed to know that Plato/ Socrates complained that words were stuck on the page, projecting himself into intense discussions centuries away; that his dialogues could not themselves *dialogue with the reader*, though he composed them in a way that they seemed

---

* Depending on how you put the date. Plato, after Socrates' death in 399 BC, held on to much of the material for decades, dying just over a half-century later, in 347 BC.

to.*

I needed then to have my own experience of actually dialoguing with text, due neither to reading the pages nor to talking face to face (or through technology) with the author, but to some location in between. In between these two choices lay the choice that was directly allied with Plato's description of communication—Socrates' despair that words

---

* Timaeus, in *Timaeus and Critias*.

Fire, he cited, filled the universe, in the form of light, and due to this we could see at all. Because something streamed through and from us, that was the same as this "soft fire" (non-burning), or light. What has this to do with us now? Or what does the language translate into, so that we might see what he really said—if we change the definitions of the terms? He said something inside us, that corresponded to the light outside, had a fire base but did not burn, and that this was present in the daylight, and also in our capacity to see and in ourselves, in inner fire, or light.

were stuck onto pages, that their communication capacity had a certain cementedness.

So, you would have to believe in the fact (which I do and did, and the result was this) that the information did not have to stay glued to the pages, or have a form it appeared *through*, in our world. It was here, regardless, and the format of the book gave it *one* structure, which I (or you, supposing you wanted to or learned how)—sensing it, attuned to it—could "pick up." Just as we pick up a stone on the ground, or any heavily materialized object. Information was just as present, especially if having been put into form *by a mind*.

But how could one directly access the information, when the brain, whose perception faculties were normally thought to require seeing, or hearing, or something at least brought by the "senses" (those we knew and numbered), was not that slippery, was it, to bypass what we counted as ways it could proceed to us? That is, in everyday terms.

Information that was external, such as in a book, reached us externally, through the book. And that was that. When not even weighable mass but intangibility itself, it was nonsense to think that it could take the form of energy and transform right into our own minds, secretly interacting with the words on the page (which communicated how? through what form of wave, leaping right over to OUR BRAIN WAVES??). If so.

Plato, after Socrates' death, held on to much of the matter for decades.* Several.

_____

* Darwin was much influenced by Goethe. Goethe wrote about "morphology"—which those recently writing on it (Rupert Sheldrake and others) posit through "self-organizing fields."

Looking at the concept that there is influence (or communication/transformation/creativity) in intangible (or latent-potential, nonmatter) form would lead to a missing development in understanding. That is, to make the human grow in size—like evolving a backbone, which is a good analogy. We grew the brain, but not the backbone—all mammals having this peculiarity. We have twenty-four CTL vertebrae (cervical, thoracic, and lumbar), "but most mammals—including animals as diverse as most rodents, rabbits, deer, kangaroos, koalas, cows, monkeys, and others—all have 26 CTL vertebrae while dogs, cats, bears, weasels, otters, and their relatives all have 27. There is little variation in these numbers either within species or across different species, even different species separated by over 160 million years of evolution." It might seem that the species that learned to walk always erect would firm up their backbone—but this is enough of that topic here ("Ecology and Evolution," https://ecoevocommunity.nature.com/posts/48312-on-the-backs-of-mammals-evolutionary-constraint-in-the-evolution-of-the-mammalian-vertebral-column). Don't get me going on such a playful topic, ripe for comment and pokes and jabs. Our backbone like that of a rodent? A rabbit. A weasel? Yea for them. Who knew?

Suppose at death one held onto nothing but a question, vowing to energize that question, wherever it might be found (and thus to find oneself again in the changing research directed toward the question. This is an example, one only).*

---

*So, I have wondered if I had written this book in another dimension. Perhaps it was the one I SAW, FELT, being written upon entering the consciousness in Zurich. Why else did I enter it AT THAT POINT— only to watch it write a book that I would not read? Not recognize— NOW. So, if I can hold still the mind and the excitement, dare to imagine that that perhaps the book being written was this one here, then I can perhaps assist as it climbs down through the "ethers," changing form all the way of course, to here, THEN, can I calm myself enough to allow this already-written material to transform itself into words here.

Not being afraid that such a movement will endanger it. Damage it.

Thus, be an accumulation of very precise references, that could be used to ask other questions. Or stop asking questions. Or be implied behind all one's experiences—which were then research, in a manner of speaking, on this prior idea.

Not daring to think then who the author is, for it is inside a technique that would first have to be explained, with the question of identity far down the list—so far that by the time one got there, it would be no question at all. Everyone could answer a question of that nature, even relating to themselves, if only keeping the emotional body fed milk—or whatever else kept it quiet, listening, assured, not racing out and shouting ludicrous things that to it seemed logical, but were not at all.

Had we frozen content and communication into concrete modes, even as we saw our technology jetting information around, defying these descriptions? Suppose we had idly stepped into this limitation. And at this time could discover that it was a brain slant, an acquired "taste." It was not the truth. Not any longer. Because it was possible to experience this supposed truth as merely a conditioned "limitation."

Then one could not so confidently hide it or suppress it in the same way. One had to make adjustments, values, draw up a new constitution. Based on these interactive principles of the human condition. Of course, it was also true, still and always, that it required a focused mind to bring a particular thought to fruition. Amazingly so, of course.

A Step Back

Einstein's "Autobiographical Notes" ("something like my own obituary") recalls himself at around five witnessing the "determined" nature of motion of the compass needle: its sense of direction; its nonreference to immediate external force, "effect connected with direct 'touch'"): "I can still remember—or at least believe I can remember—" he wrote, "that this experience made a deep and lasting impression upon me. Something deeply hidden had to be behind things. What man sees before him from infancy causes no reaction of this kind; he is not surprised over the falling of bodies, concerning wind and rain, nor concerning the moon or about the fact that the moon does not fall down, nor concerning the differences between living and non-living matter" (pp. 577, 580 in Ferris, ed.).

I see what I have been struggling with. Why things feel incomplete, when perhaps I should let go. It is because of this **further step.**

CHAPTER FOUR

Reflections on a Theory of Organisms

20

Holism in Biology

Bohr's method versus the historical method extended from Descartes: "Similarity" versus "replication." On conservation of properties.

"Recall now in what the Cartesian Method consists: It claims that one should deal with complex systems by analyzing them into smaller and simpler components and study these components individually, putting them mentally together again at the end. Clearly, the Cartesian Method fails . . . because it is inadequate, in the case of complementary relationships." (p. 101), which is where the Bohr Method comes in.

What distinguishes the Bohr Method is that in the case of "wholes" (organisms), the great physicist and teacher of the graduate student Elsasser, "generally considered the father of atomic theory, . . . speaks on occasion of a 'renunciation of knowledge'" (p. 9).

One of the points this is leading to is, "We do not as yet claim to know 'how much' of the behavior of an organism is due to mechanistically explicable causality and 'how much' is due to creativity."

He goes on: "that if one defines the non-mechanical powers of the organism in terms of holistic memory one introduces essentially a novel *conservative* element, where the entity conserved is information" (p. 118).

A few steps away, defining "transfer of information," he arrives at the Rule of repetition: "*Holistic information transfer involves in the first approximation the reproduction of states or processes that have existed previously in the individual or species, as the case may be*" (p. 119).

"The basic underlying assumption is that information can be transferred by holistic behavior *without spatio-temporal contiguity*. It is therefore an entirely new way of looking at nature which has no counterpart in the quantitative physical sciences."

He compares this leap to the leap Newton was unprepared to take willingly (and physicists after him) in wondering about "action at a distance" (i.e., how something was interacted with at a distance, without some medium of transfer of information (p. 120), or some "inscription (storage of a message)" (p. 116).

Drastically simplifying the explanation after defining it technically, he labels the culprit, the thing responsible: "creativity" (p. 120)

CHAPTER FOUR (CONT'D).

Were Newton alive, continuing his research, he might bolt upright, with the idea that perhaps here was some insight to that question he took to his grave. Moved to the biological reams, action through empty space was contemplatable, if we, or rather Elsasser, could find, on the molecular level, something quite tasteful called "creativity," based on the "systematic breaking-down of ordinary molecular causality," and further, that exact replication was not involved, some of the time, but *similarity* of one thing to the thing "reproduced" (p. 120). Needless to say, this is vastly condensed, dipped into, so not to be too overwhelming.

X IS THIS TRUE?

Little Carl Jung, with a scant handful of years on the Earth, between the ages of four and five, was already ready to contribute. Descending through a "dark, rectangular stone-lined hole" in his first remembered dream, he entered an underground chamber. What soon enough caught his eye there was a sumptuous, golden throne on which sat a tall bloblike figure afflicted with a rigid eye perched on top of what would be its head, the head undifferentiated as to face and hair. It was "the man-eater," he heard as the "creature" stared fixedly upward.

Likewise—four years later in Earth chronology—Little Einstein, at about age five, encountered the compass, eliciting from him the response that there was something mysterious in life the adult world paid scant attention to. As a man, he wondered what the world would look like if seen from a sunbeam.

The Unconscious was ramping up with discoveries for us, working through these two child minds.

In earlier writings, I drew an empathetic parallel between the child Jung and the child (myself) at the piano at seven, unable to finish her first recital (a Bach barcarolle) except through returning repeatedly to the beginning, concluding in one final straight-through, start-to-finish success. In playing, almost hypnotized though frightened, the repeated cycles, where did she/I go, on another level? (According to Hermann Minkowski, Einstein's famous mathematics professor, a thin sliver of each person's time, or "imaginary time," intersected— "wiggled through"—the whens and wheres of world time. He *called it a world line.*) Stepping out further into the "underground," encaved connected threads, we bring this up here.

For playing the piece, I was given a bust of Beethoven. For years, taking the cue from my seven-year-old self, I thought it was Mozart.

Such was only the beginning of the haunting questions this dream left Jung with (p. 26, *Memories, Dreams, Reflections*). More up ahead.

But Einstein was not interested in math at the time; he skipped most of his lectures. As Minkowski himself told Born, *"in his student days Einstein had been a real lazybones. He never bothered about mathematics at all."* Einstein confirms this in his Autobiographical Notes: "I *had excellent teachers (for example, Hurwitz, Minkowski), so that I should have been able to obtain a mathematical training in depth. I worked most of the time in physical laboratory, however, fascinated by the direct contact with experience. The balance of the time I used, in the main, in order to study at home the works of Kirchhoff, Helmholtz, Hertz, etc."*[12]

And so Penelope continued to weave: the back-to-back child tales, that though not unusual per se, if taken up into archetypical contours, certainly in my case, seemed to outline, sketch, roadmap the structure of a life, where child after child was imprinted or impregnated with the sense of something beyond what the parents' world was functioning in; some basic fundamental. What???

Fitting the piece of "me," as anyone can, into the larger ideological framework impregnating these other children, whose initial insight "wiggled" into the world timeline, strongly helping shape the world view, would be bound to lead somewhere—to any who tried it! Let's go on. Pushing the way open, to—? Jung associated the "creature" with something that "might crawl off the throne like a worm and creep towards me"; raising the question if somewhere in the collective there was the study of a WORMHOLE.

Jung's dream, symbolizing the unfoldment of his life's work, he said, was still alive, still active. No, I do not jest—in the role of jester cast though I might be.

Almost room-high, tree-trunk-thick, the throne was highlighted by "an aura of light"—the details providing a reappearing theme for many, turning over new ruminations on it; this instance is no exception.*

---

* As if Jung were illustrating, holding for him—a bit of confirming data—the young Freud's incipient phallic theory, in a symbol, as would be typical of Jung.

Leonard Shlain uses the provocative phraseology that early humans did not "think" but only perceived.

Hiding the throne was a "green curtain," Jung said.

Shall we, while jester-cast, comment that "green" is *"vert"* (in French), with a silent "t," as "worm" is *"vers"* (not pronouncing the "s"). BUT *"verser"* (pronounced *"verre,* or "glass," say) is TO POUR.

We are IN TROY
in the ramparts as the besieging begins
in the Beginning of the Century
in the Voyage Home
We are in the HOME-
Eric
Tradition
We are with the
ancient
Singers
Sewers from the celestial
traditions
Casting words and rhyme down through the air like pollen,
to make us
FLOUR
DOUGH

We are in the
OVER-
seers section
in the
noncontributing supposedly inter-
ACTION
We are in the Insti-
gation
situation
Now, let us enter the arena of full-fledged
participation
DiagNOSE
the prescriptions for cures
Let us do it

Quick, then, while no one observes
Let us do it,
seed the Earth with some
IDEA
BULBS

Bulbs of Light, we plant here then
bulb them
In lieu of bombs that could be used
let us send down some
BULBS
of light
Let us send electricity containers, let us
send them bulbs of
Light
In the garden, where planted and tended, the
Light was in bulbs, to be harvested and grown
and now these groans let through the universe show us
the locations where these bulbs planted deep
are ready to be
turned on

and so the delegation and the contingents overseeing
in their look-out nooks
that spread vastly over the areas
that were larger than one-person, two-person, three-person width
these contingents of overlooking, overseeing
as if peacock FANS
single structures
did intend to join the ranks
of—or was it lend a hand to?—
Woman/Man

up-and-down wavelike
Air
symbol
beggar at the window[*]
sig/*arête* in my pocket—any pocket—asked for
to light
disturbances
in the atmosphere
close behind
that this the time the Air Pockets
are in every journey
POCKETS
Packets
Get them
They are ON

———————————

[*] If this reference is meaningless, nothing to fear. He is lavishly reintroduced in the pages 105ff, and so as not to spoil that reintroduction there, let us just race past that glancing seed. A blur that swept past the vision so quickly it registered only subliminally, if at all, as we catch him musing down here in the subterranean.

Or was he (the beggar at the window) saying that he got left "behind" by going faster than (or nearing) the speed of light. Then he was invisible. Not because he didn't have light, but there was nothing to reflect in the mirror, because of the speed, unless maybe a very thin vertical line, and now standing outside the windowpane, the glass, if he reflected himself, the return visit likewise meant his field dissolved, so he would stand in an arriving field. He had managed to get here. But his field—where was it? Was he saying he needed, in order to make his speech heard, not light—the medium (in this case and in code, cigarette) as something to light; the modality, the concrete, the physical. So as to make himself visible. Something to interact with! He knew he was real, he had real facts, or "fracts, that no one else did. No, he metaphorically needed a cigarette—something to light with his Light, to enter- ACT
With.

Even more imaginative, philosophical reasonings came to me later, as each option acquired a context. As if, and why not, a "mirror reality" could be something "reflected" into a part of the self.

THE WAY

I open a biography of Kappellmeister Mozart Not while writing. Many months afterwards——while proofreading. Mozart himself describes how he composes. The author places him in—a carriage setting, en route to Prague:

> I really can say no more on this subject than the following; for I myself know no more about it, and cannot account for it. When I am, as it were, completely myself, entirely alone, and of good cheer—say, travelling in a carriage, or walking after a good meal, or during the night when I cannot sleep; it is on such occasions that my ideas flow best and most abundantly. *Whence* and *how* they come, I know not; nor can I force them. Those ideas that please me, I retain in memory, and am accustomed, as I have been told, to hum them to myself . . .
>
> All this fires my soul, and provided I am not disturbed, my subject enlarges itself, becomes methodized and defined, and the whole, though it be long, stands almost complete and finished in my mind, so that I can survey it, like a fine picture, or a beautiful statue, at a glance. Nor do I hear in my imagination the parts *successively*, but I hear them, as it were, *gleich alles zusammen*, all at once.

All this inventing, then, all this producing, absorbed Wolfgang in the coach. Sometimes he reached absently for the door-*pocket*, took out his case of illegible scrap-papers and jotted down a theme or phrase [last italics added] (p. 283, Davenport).

Now that we are this far along, we can say that this loading up of the book (not intended, for it was slim) suddenly comes because the End again, that will be full of surprises, is partly known to us. So, as we reread we are aware that the End refused to come singly, but with a troop of like vintage and nature. And so, the level

Xfrom   which it

revealed itself comes in a full shell. A chamber, a full "round." A "shot" (heard round the world). A shot GLASS that broke the mirror. That made the break "thru.'" Fourfold and SEVEN, it was. FourFOLD. And seven . . . Pileups, the system of universe pileups. We were in it now. Could we see the picture, as Mozart outlined the procedure??? It was no more difficult in words than in music. It was the same procedure. A diagram. That much, just a dia-GRAM. FourFOLD. And SEVEN!

So the markup continued.
And the countDOWN
the markUP
AND THE COUNT-
Down

Surely it wasn't a Mozart CARRY-

AGE

Be-

tween   two train cars, was it a Mozart Carriage

It was a throne, in the dream. NOT A TRENCH. It could have been pictured

AS A TRENCH. An entrenched idea.

Part Three

CHAPTER FIVE

In Tracing the Vanishing Act

$\mathcal{I}$n tracing the Vanishing Act of rational reality, Arthur Koestler begins the sequence of steps (let us listen to him, as he might have talked to J. B. Rhine, way back in 1961, on Galileo's and Descartes' banishment of the "secondary" qualities, "the very essence of the sensual world—colour and sound, heat, odour, and taste—from the realm of physics to that of subjective illusion," page 539, *The Sleepwalkers*).

Galileo wrote, "'I think that if ears, tongues and noses were removed, shapes and numbers and motions would remain, but not odours or tastes or sounds. The latter, I believe, are nothing more than names when separated from living beings'" (ibid., p. 476).

In the next two centuries "Each of the 'ultimate' and 'irreducible' primary qualities of the world of physics proved in its turn to be an illusion. The hard atoms of matter went up in fireworks; the concepts of substance, force, of effects determined by causes, and ultimately the very framework of space and time turned out to be as
illusory as the 'tastes, odours, and colours' which Galileo had treated so contemptuously" (p. 540).

> But it is doubtful whether it is permissible to say that the electron "occupies space" at all. Atoms have the capacity of swallowing

energy and of spitting out energy—in the form of light rays, for instance. When a hydrogen atom, the simplest of all, with a single electron-planet, swallows energy, the planet jumps from its orbit to a larger orbit—say, from the orbit of Earth to the orbit of Mars; when it emits energy, it jumps back again into the smaller orbit. But these jumps are performed by the planet without it passing through the space that separates the two orbits. It somehow de-materializes in orbit A and rematerializes in orbit B. Moreover, since the amount of "action" performed by the hydrogen electron while going once round its orbit is the indivisibly smallest quantum of action (Planck's basic constant "h"),* it is meaningless to ask at what precise point of its orbit the

---

* Max Planck, in solving the so-called ultraviolet catastrophe, which predicted that any "blackbody," for example, an oven, should emit energy that approached infinity—a ghastly prediction that promised we would all burn alive each time we turned our stove on—realized that would not be the case if he posited the then-mind-bending hypothesis that light radiated in sizes, discovering the indicator "h," the very smallest unit of energy, or action, a rare constant like the speed of light; he "came to the conclusion that the frequency distribution of black body radiation could only be accounted for if the radiation was emitted as separate 'packets' called quanta, rather than continuously." Einstein jumped in, concurring, naming the "packet of electromagnetic radiation" a photon. More on this in the text proper pronto (p. 531, *Oxford Family Encyclopedia*).

electron is at a given moment of time. It is equally everywhere. (p. 541)*

He quotes Bertrand Russell, that matter "is a convenient formula for describing what happens where it isn't" (page 542). So "beams of electrons, . . . supposedly elementary particles of matter," behave like *now* bullets, or lumps, and *now* waves:

But waves in, on, of what? A wave is movement, undulation; but what is it that moves and undulates, producing my chair? It

---

* At every command that would require the screen to shift, the computer first broke up all the text into geometric forms and then, as with a smile, a demonstration to a child, reassembled all the text into the readable, familiar linear passages. Again and again, the burst of geometric form intercepted the shift from linear text to next linear text. The pages became kaleidoscopic playgrounds. A snap and a presto, and then on to the next familiar linear standstill. And then snap and presto, and a moment's unblurred revisitation of this type energy.

is nothing the mind can conceive of, not even
empty space, for each

ace
line
the
ous
n a
pp.

electron requires a three-dimensional sp
s need six dimensions, three electrons r
ist. In some sense these waves [in
on] are real; we can photograph the fam
ley produce when they pass through
ley are like the grin of the Cheshire cat" (

empty space, for each electron requires a three-dimensional space for itself, two electrons need six dimensions, three electrons nine dimensions, to co-exist. In some sense these waves [in the wave/particle alternation] are real; we can photograph the famous dart-board pattern they produce when they pass through a diffraction grate; yet they are like the grin of the Cheshire cat" (pp. 541–542).

So Max Planck studied the heat (energy) in an oven, *discovering it distributed itself related to its frequency.*

Planck's "equation, relating the energy of a quantum to its frequency, is the basis of quantum theory." He revealed that **action** *comes in sizes* (quanta)—h" being the smallest.

Now, "h" sometimes appears with a horizontal bar across the top to indicate a further step, a division, in the equation standing for the ratio, "the proportionality constant," between "the energy of the packets and the frequency." More, a high-frequency wave could receive a high-frequency packet of energy. But not so, a low-frequency wave. It could not (E = hv)!! Meaning if we raise our frequency, we can receive more energy. (But not if we don't.) This is beautifully discussed in "The Granularity of the World: Quanta" in *Helgoland: Making Sense of the Quantum World*, by Rovelli.

All the steps, the "packets," of an event, could be bundled, coming in quick succession or almost on top of one another. But even so, there was an incrementality. One could enter an event at any point. Beginning and end did actually exist. Down on the smallest level, where things below eye level swarmed and hinted to us of their existence. And therefore action, yours and mine, is measurable piecemeal—a bit of action plus another bit; it is not all or nothing. But, as we experience it in steps, lo and behold, that's how it is in energy, which is to say—a further bit to chew on—an action is dividable..

These things, shaking up the complacency and inertia—the sense of things continuing as usual—stated, in various forms the need to prepare, to look ahead, as always when something could be met on either side of the outcome.

So, which did the Earth want—wars perpetuated *into space*? The same lessons, pushed into *even larger proportions*? Did it want to be the passive participant, surprised by the troubles it found itself in, looking backward at the lessons it had not noticed, not heeded? Or something new? Did it want to step into leadership? to be a planet that taught others, supposing we found them or, if not, taught at home? How did one best meet these radically shifting circumstances?? One could stock up and make sure supplies were in sufficient amounts—defensively. OR transform the reaction mechanism.

One could be prepared. Quickly switch to anticipation. Try to offer the most possible positive attractions—vibrations into space, expected fruitful events ahead. Stop everything and turn attention to the atmospheric forecasts the Earth was creating, in sending out its expectations in the tiny trails of the future that were making their way in.

In fact, have we been given a key to burn away this

Earth karma?

Did the "new births" have to be another dimension, relative to the Earth? Those who carried the new dimensions (or didn't, but got too close) have to have a physical death, get close and yet have to be born in another dimension? Or—!!!!! The Death of the Old bringing in, in its not-wake but on its very STERN (OR STERNE) the Other Dimension Birth. Of the Old Earth and its young integration of ideas? That is, on the landing now. What kind?

An airplane landing on a runway? A stairs—with, one landing up, the consciousness unable to make its presence seen as that.

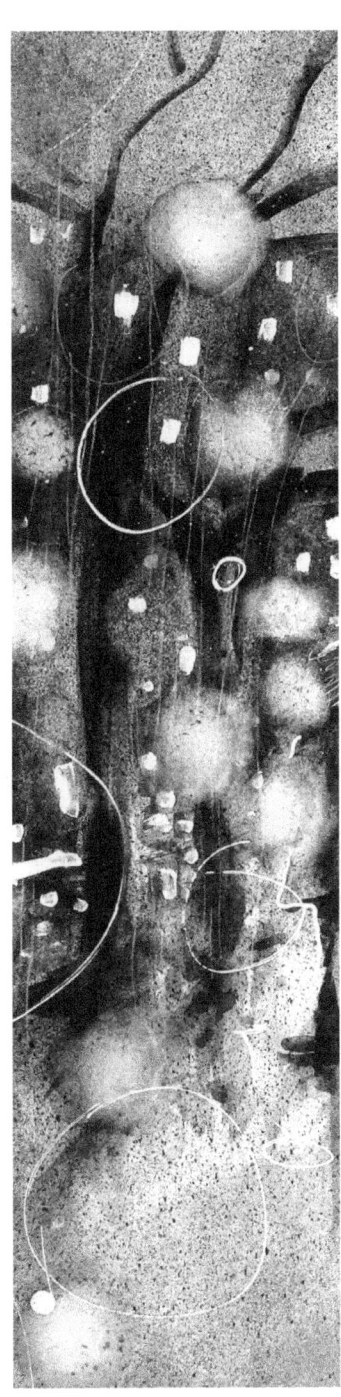

Part Four

CHAPTER SIX

Sitting at the Bistro du Dôme

Sitting at the
Bistro du Dôme, thirty-two years later, after I began
in 1965 the *Love in Transition* series *there*, watching through
the window . . . No clown, no new symbolic
action, where once long ago a beggar, outside a window,

used

MIME.*

---

* Another place where we ratchet up and gather together the threads introduced before, thereby requiring that the new visitor have a backward anchor into time, which would be the Dôme bistro in Paris, France, at the moment of watching the beggar that we are just about to examine more closely, for his value in stepping into the concrete dimension (as a symbol); at that moment (as he stepped out of what capsule, or cubicle) this series was first begun (if not in wish to write it, the wish being firmly set in place decades earlier). Triggered here with a Now BEGIN in 1965—the beggar acting out subliminally to me a unit of "action"—that, however (or how? ever?), had a great triggering value in the symbolic mind. Again, why? Let's keep on this trail.

rbC

C

The recognition undoubtedly carried a ritual knowledge to the part of the brain that understands rituals.

I did not go to the deathbed of **Milton Klonsky sixteen years later.** But mirroring itself in a practically simultaneous **PARADE**, it came to me. The absent physical

location replaced by its meaning in
another location. Level 2. That symbolic enactment, I could
comprehend and unroll.

For I was from now on going to be apprised of nonphysical
occurrences, those that existed *inside the physical ones.* My dimension
now, for years to come.

An event—a death—so able to represent itself that there
before my physical eyes, it showed itself as all that was important
to it (also to me, evidently) in that moment, on that day (and
many days ahead); that it clothed itself *that day* in a band that,
playing its drums and other instruments, brandished large signs
associating it with—Neptune. But I honed in on one image: *"the
end of the* BLOCK." It mimed its significance, reversing its march
at—as if canceling out—THE END OF THE BLOCK. Then paraded
right back in front of me. At the moment it was in front of me the
second time, my pocketbook strap—oddly, I thought—turned
inside out.

Did events always represent themselves this way? Always bring
some message, some coded meaning from some dimension?
Here was another area of solution-potential WE DID NOT KNOW
ABOUT yet lived in a world comprised of it. Some consciousness
which always "read" life like this? And we had that consciousness
dormant IN US!! I apparently did.

At *this* death, of Milton Klonsky in 1981, the version I happened
to step into, at just that imaged connection, the Alpha returned to
the Omega of that trajectory; in apparent, mysterious triumph—
the march alive with pep, a secret victory it joyously celebrated.
Widely known somewhere, it marched in open acknowledgment
of this feat. Only, I stood there alone, not even at that moment
knowing what I saw—except sensing the announcement of victory.

This ancient seagod, said Plato—or Critias for him—had
been given the island kingdom Atlantis. What has it to do with
this marching band, after all this time? We do not know. But we
are getting closer. A parade, not into Jerusalem, but where? in
what kind, what locale, what particular, "heaven"? Ticktocking
moments, and we followed some ticking, at just

the right "time."

1L

I, watching its *dimensional* significance,

*bOW

OW

(S2Q

all the marchers, not seeing names or faces. Not connecting it to the faraway, New York City to be exact, thing it represented, but to—an obstacle surmounted. Archetypically, like the stone rolled away from the tomb and Mary Magdalene being immediately alerted.

He had said to me, "Is all that came come after this dot dot dot"—wearily when our relationship seemed blocked. Ah, blocked.

I add to that—this day, so many years later—the dot dot dot that CAME FROM

Plato.
    his wax tablet
    papyrus sheet—

The Atlantis story.
Atlanta, the
    cigar-
    Rhet.
    Stopped—
    BLOCKED—
    0W

when Critias, without further notice, not even finishing the last sentence in Plato's book, did *not continue* his explanation about the fate of humankind; left unreported how it disintegrated, *as it had not while more than half divine*, sired by Neptune to a mortal.

Just as the story was picking up (steam or whatever in those days) and Zeus was going to issue punishment, Plato stopped writing.

Whether, as some sources assert, he never wrote further or, as others believe, he wrote but the text was lost, there is a gap here in history.

*rbC

The parade brought a transmission, a movie in another dimension!!—without the REALITY OF WHICH the rest of my life would have remained off-track, from its highest—presently activating itself, so that now finally I can see it—purpose. No one, *including myself*, would ever have known. How would I have found a place ever again, to get into my own future, destiny, sense of the reality of **lifetime** moments? As now, helping with the computer. He did not take my reality away

closer. Banged on the door of my brain by
the things it held most reliable.

eath. He brought it

ng away its fixtures,

at d
takii

at death. He brought it closer. Banged on the door of my brain by taking away its fixtures, the things it held most reliable.

For if I had not seen the parade, felt it signified something, I would not have set out to investigate and thus not had the resulting initiations, starting in Zurich. The long-ago Paris beggar, who announced the show was about to begin, can now be placed side by side with the conclusive marching parade in 1981, where the curtain went down on the physical lifetime of Milton Klonsky, while I watched, unalerted by anyone as to what it meant on this other energy/symbol stage.

That all revealed/correlated by journal notes later. The parading band (the SONS AND DAUGHTERS OF NEPTUNE, their signs read), permitting only that glimpse, as if it and it only would take me into that other dimension as they passed that particular corner. I surely was ignorant of the nearly simultaneous event, that same day (hour?) November 29, in a hospital bed in New York.

Or that on that same day (years earlier) Enrico Fermi died. Which might at least bring into synchronicity the documentary series of Robert Oppenheimer, *et al*, that ran on my TV set-- dramatizing the Manhattan Project's creation of the atomic bomb—during the weeks just before the death that I knew nothing (I thought) consciously of, though unconsciously yes, I was guessing loud and clear. (In my private code, I'd applied "Manhattan Project" to my New York City internage with Klonsky, and for that matter the other two big-figure males in my twenties escapades in Manhattan. A reverse sort of Manhattan Project, of course.)

Similarly, in Virginia *during* my mother's death, a *Yellow Rose* TV episode mimicked the car chase she was dying in right then or nearly, to the on-screen theme song "There's a yellow rose in Texas . . . ," tears welling up in my eyes for no known reason—my mother's name was Rose.

NOTE: Synchronicity, according to Jung, both connected things in time and also was of the clairvoyant spatial sort, though it was mostly the time sort that we noted down. He especially pointed out the subjective/objective synchronicity of two things that (one subjective and the other an outer, objective manifestation) indicated the same meaning. This another sign of the trail we are on.

The Universe, most definitely, was self-aware. It knew what was going on inside it, though whether we can call it "conscious" is another matter if an observer, a holder of the awareness, is required for consciousness. Is the Universe enough of an observer, or does it have to be more than radio waves and sound waves and electricity and such that holds the consciousness to call it that? Does mind have to come into play, and can mind be just these energies beyond the visible spectrum in our terms? No, the Universe operates in a larger spectrum, a larger consciousness. Whose?

Years later, it seems I have entered the **most subtle** future of that moment—given a chance for it to have a future (else, I become the block in its path), when a thing, apparently in one place, in reality is, at least in some dimension of itself, also (or in that dimension only) in another (making me something trans-subsisting between the two dimensions, or whatever they are, MERELY THROUGH THE LIFETIME OF THAT ONE MOMENT. Allowing it a parallel lifetime to mine, or in mine, which was easy in this case. Thus, the symbol, sole representative of the future of *that*

moment.

*b0W

—the physical could not hold

it, too 1

acking in clues, spread out,

though old (mind you).

For here we are, on the borderline of an understanding in which things *superimpose*—this moment on top of that one. Patterns are made here. Combinations. Those juxtapositions refer to each other.

After all my speculation, now comes this confounding statement, which I briefly referred to many pages back:

> Not only can two events be correlated, linking the earlier one to the later one, but *two events can become correlated such that it becomes impossible to say which is earlier and which is later.* Each of these events is the cause of the other, as if each were the first to occur. (Even a single observer can encounter this causal ambiguity, so it's distinct from the temporal reversals that can happen when two observers move at different velocities, as described in Einstein's special theory of relativity.) . . .
>
> "If you have space-time, you have a well-defined causal order," said Časlav Grukner, a physicist at the University of Vienna who studies quantum information. But "if you don't have a well-defined causal order," he said—as is the case in experiments he has proposed—then "you don't have space-time." Some physicists take this as evidence for a profoundly nonintuitive worldview, in which quantum correlations are more fundamental than space-time and space-time itself is somehow built up from correlations among event, in what might be called quantum relationalism. The argument updates [seventeenth-century scientist/mathematician] Gottfried Leibniz and [turn-of-the-twenty-first-century physicist] Ernst Mach's idea that space-time might not be a God-given backdrop to the

world, but instead might derive from the material
contents of the universe. [13] (emphasis added)

So then when I falteringly (convinced on the inside) years
earlier speculated—sure it was accurate—on the existence
of "event balls," when there seemed to the naked eye no
connection, the participants never having met, I was not
speaking from some Outer Galaxy about impossibilities and
woo woo ideas: *events somehow could be predicated on other events*
over time. Dramatic events in my own life had raised in me
this incredible speculation.

No, not incredible, the above quotation says, confirming
that it's very likely in the quantum-entangled world, which
our world exists in, that these things do "hook up," based
on, to our eyes, likenesses that are so subtle or seemingly
inconsequential we would pay them no mind. They might
even, taking it further, I had detected, based on my own
life, "hook up" in a relay race of "Go" signals. Like a lineup
of quanta strung together? Like a Christmas decoration?
In an Other World cause-effect where the triggering of one
triggers the whole piñata though not in our sense of time, just
(probably) in a set sequence. A string? Or a resonating series
of quanta lumps????? Scary. Scary. Scary. How can we stand
to not know so much about our living conditions? Our world?
Our potential powers? The consciousness we left dangling in
the winds, puffing up our unconscious.

※

Once, sitting in the Royal Chapel of Versailles Palace,
meditating, my feet on marble floors, my head far below the
vaulted ceiling, I felt the past reach out with a message for me,
a sense of former inhabitants of Versailles making contact,
whether it was just old "memories" residing in the walls
or a presence. Telling me *not to judge them*. Did I think them
trivial? Don't. Without an extreme, perhaps even negative,

form one person walked in, we could not create patterns that incorporated a portion of it. Look at the panoply of variety peopled by this flashy court in this ornate setting. In that instant, I realized the humanity of this aristocratic Louis XIV court in all its color. Look at these flawed lifetimes, each as a rich, picturesque, intensely lived form humanity now had, to draw from. How less rich we would be without them "in the pot."

As the walls of my brain feel the reality that says it is stronger than the one outside, it must be that I am inside—or am I in some relation to?—a SUPER
POSITION.

Or am I just inside the passagewa

ys back to me, going through the corridors of time backwards, as each thing that was important in the past becomes so, stays so; is imprinted in me once again. And this time I will not forget.

Is time, then a closed fist?

"I am myself and my circumstances," I quoted to Klonsky, compliments of Ortega y Gasset.

He quipped, booming the words out in one of the treasured sayings I packed away for later:

"No! The colors change. But the Dome remains the same."

Was, this time period on the Earth now, the DOME TOO going to change? And did it have something to do with the signal entering my brain in 1965—Bingo! Begin! The subliminal signal to start the book, long detoured around, scurried around, as the momentum built.

The Montparnasse beggar scene, flocked, one might imagine, by a burgeoning history of artists that frequented the café, it set the time in NOW, awakened the "unit of action," the cluster, or very precise instruction—from where? The "prearranged" signal finding its path into time. Because, if thinking of units of action in a nontime-bound "location," then the players could "gravitate" around something other than Earth time. Yes or no? Of course, yes.

The concrete scene, at the Dôme Cafe—further—cross-related with the above saying, later to be cryptically added to the small collection of clues?? And all that, my brain already knew where to store and how to interpret? I liked the idea. Was the Earth DOME going to change??? in this period??? this "transition"?????

What was the big overarching thing, symbolized by Dome, that never changed in spite of differing colors/frequencies it lived inside, the contexts, but now would? Was it a spectrum we operated in that restricted the whole??? Was there an archetype (or many archetypes), tying down the dome to the usual range of colors, even though they were not fixed, but shifted, if speed accelerated to immense rates? (A way to approach asking the question.)

Across the window, outlining the wavy line with his bobbing head, the beggar hinted to me, in the clearest silence possible, look at this sine wave; that he was standing in a wave. Now "collapsed," these many years later:

—SINE LANGUAGE.

"Waves in general [in quantum mechanics] are superpositions of simple waves [of possibility], which are known as sine waves (p. 67, *The Visionary Window*: A *Quantum Physicist's Guide to Enlightenment*).

An "electron possibility wave" is "technically called a wave packet" (p. 33).

So, there it was, IN BLACK AND WHITE.

So, alright already. What did it mean? LIGHT that not in a great voice spoke, but pantomimed, working through the SINE language, of—was it a great Earth WAVE? A WAVE OF UNCONSCIOUSNESS, trying to become conscious to us? Our Ulysses in the END, HIS RETURN HOME. An archetype, yes.

Now, at this distance, so clearly that. Why so urgent, then, first glimpsed, in this one location, in 1965??? A beggar's sine wave (or wavy line across plate glass), across a window of time and possibility?

Asking for a cigarette from a Packet.

It is an overstatement to say that all things are interconnected in quantum mechanics. If that were true in any substantial way, we could not do any calculation in quantum mechanics without involving all the objects in the universe. The correct statement is that all things are potentially interconnected. As waves, quantum objects spread in possibility: so if we wait awhile, there will be overlap—interconnection. And for macro-objects the spreading is very slow, so interconnection in this sense would take a long time.

In science within consciousness, the interconnection occurs via consciousness. Consciousness, via intention, can correlate two objects, two brains, and collapse similar actualities in both. There is now experimental evidence of interconnection that supports this view, thanks to the work of Mexican neurophysiologist Jacobo Grinberg-Zylberbaum and his collaborators.

In this experiment, two subjects become correlated by meditating together with the intention of establishing direct communication. After being instructed to maintain direct communication, they are separated, put in electromagnetically insulated chambers, and wired up to separate electroencephalogram (EEG) machines. When one of them sees a series of light flashes, which produces an evoked potential in his brain's EEG, a transferred potential similar in phase and strength to the evoked potential is found in the other subject's EEG as well. Control subjects, however, do not show a transferred potential. The conclusion is straightforward: consciousness collapses similar states of actualities in both brains because the brains are correlated via conscious intention (p. 69, enlargement added).

So alright already again. A bobbing line (like for apples, presumably the one that Newton saw fall) across the glass from end to end. Pack ready to be lit. A plan, even, but across a barrier. Someone standing there—in the standing wave?—CONSCIOUS OF IT!

Whereas on the other side of the window was the unconscious position, the one I sat in, but at least more conscious at that moment than most.

How many centuries of line-up in the packet, and not a material witness on the other side of the window, in what we called reality? But something was timed for now, or could be, and it required going into the packet! Not that I gave him the cigarette, right then. But what I did give the beggar's plight, his signal, was *attention*.

Standing there, garbed like Ulysses at the end of his voyage, hoping Penelope would recognize him, hoping home had been safeguarded in his absence, after long journeying, now HOME, wanting to

get the message across.

Yes, *straight across* the window he had bobbed his head up and down, making the imaginary smoke rings—trying to get his message across!

Where in fact does that put us??? signaling in glass was signaling in what used to be sand, the sands of time? Coming in?

I left the Dôme Bistro in 1965. What hop skip and jump would put me next, figuratively using "stones" to cut out the sidetracks, back in my apartment in New York, entering the rather famous Corner Bistro in Greenwich Village? Where the "delivery" occurred. There, I found the stranger Klonsky, surrounded by puffs of chain-smoked cigarettes, who was to fill me up with these wisdoms, and never noticed that in French "corner" is *"coin,"* (like Coin of the Realm) but which there also was, associatively, announcing itself loud and clear: coincidence.

Corner. *Coin.* Coincidence. End of the BLOCK. (Block BUSTER. Karma buster???)

If distance can be crossed in "no

time," space might be thought

to be crossed in *"anti-"* content.

That is, in space without "m

atter." That space could be "collapsed," even as questions (suspended in time) can be "collapsed." Even a "wave" length. One could refine this, by saying that time could be thought of as multi-present,*

---

* But connecting two points in one's personal time plan, one sometimes found the intervening time gone. And staying with the feeling, intensifying it, sensing what had been, remaining with the senses, letting them bring back the evidence, one realized, or felt that, NO TIME HAD PASSED between these two instants. As in a Time Collapse. A space collapse. Two points in time that failed to obey linear time; that acted as if time were unlabeled dots which could be moved side by side if potent enough; i.e., if filled with the energy of WHERE THEY HAD BEEN.
What they had convoyed into the present. As if the surroundings were overwhelmed by this sense of time, the past resonating with the present, the second point. As if the rest of time, all around, had amnesia, and all memory was concentrated on these two points, re-membering how alike they were, bringing the past into the moment, with no interference!! The rest was deactivated, de-energized. The energy flocked to the two points holding time like a hammock for the memory they mutually recognized the similarity of; or was it the meaning thus created IF THESE TWO POINTS NOW RECOGNIZED what was latent energy in the past that was now

Exploding with Recognition.

in different degrees of presentness. Obviously, of course. THUS: these implications, uninscribed relative to the present as the present, could be considered not "future" in the sense of nonexistent yet, but rather as at a "distance" that a *technology of the mind could cross*. Crossing it might affect its content, because interacting with it; bringing it into, at the least, a different intensity.*

---

* The cellular level is receiving direct access to the spiritual level, we have somehow deduced (we will say how, later). [No, she won't. She anticipated me here, suggesting what I might say in opening.] In directly receiving the information, it jumps quickly, in the way the body otherwise perhaps could not. Without explaining its justification. It is aligned, it knows. It does not say WHAT WITH. It does not let us have the privilege of testing the information. It takes us with it (as we were wont in the past to take it along!). Now the tables turn. It takes us.

Of course, we could refuse, object. But we sense, with the remaining authority left us, that it is correct—that it is receiving shorthand integration. We will learn how indue time. [No. This was the beginning of receding. Losing the first contact with the body's information. Aware of that. Calling oneself still the primary and only body personality, but aware that though without a channel to oneself, there was something else—call it the cells—that had first access to the information received by the body. And that it was clear, whenever this was occurring.

[Never guessing that in fact, one was receding from the present. The lifetime. That one was passing one's new self, in the dark. That it was all set up to evolve fairly smoothly.]

It is like, for whatever reason, setting out, with an unseen guide. Who hasn't the time to be introduced. But who shows us, by working inside our mind and environment and in retrospect, that the awarenesses and actions are good. So, we have enough to decide with. We say yes. We know we will be glad of it. And off, in the far unknown, past cellular "accompliceship," we go. We will report back, as always, what the inner shift—now on the cellular level—has taught us. For we are the first, the tenth, the billionth of many. This shift can take place without our acknowledgment and you push into, once again, the unconscious. But I did not want that. I wanted to enter the twenty-first century, as to enter death, with EYES WIDE OPEN.

[So here is where the personality's willingness to go further, to understand, to pass through the breakthrough, met the aforementioned human themes. Those introduced as baffling, consternating experiences of the present personality, the one going ahead by leaving her old self behind. We are speaking in so many book references here that we hope the reader will "bear" with us, while we get the variant threads into one well-woven blanket, as secure as any ever held onto by Linus.]

CHAPTER SEVEN

So, this I *am told . . .*

So this I am. I am told this upon its arrival. Its arrival, I call my birth.

—but I cannot go on here because *this* paragraph (one I highly prize) has already been published—lifted out of *this* manuscript where it lounged in obscurity for twenty-five long years, in piles of loose pages *it was unlikely* I'd *ever get to*. Most unlikely.

And I surely would not have except for a dire illness, which propelled me into a shift, 2022, canceling all predictions, all certainties. For the better, I might add. Not that many people have read the prized-by-me paragraphs in question, but they simply cannot reappear in this manuscript, the original location, as book energy does not work like that. It has to be "refreshed."

Looking at the results half a year after the first news of my illness, I call it a "makeover," a firm push into a realization of my mortality, which, oddly enough perhaps, I have never really given much credence or thought to. But a timer can be set up to convince us mortals that Earth life one day will come to a screeching halt. And so, it happened to me in 2022. And the thoughts that accompanied it were not at all what I'd have predicted. (Thankfully.) No, I had entirely different reactions: turned away from fear and gloom and toward—in fact, *this* me, who was hovering on the outskirts, saying: "Now *it's* **my** *turn*."

So that passage I pinched and pilfered for another book

really belongs right here. What to do? It established that "I" am here. This "I." This is the place I first established it, announced it, building my presence from here. But who cares to have me belabor the birth process? Who is curious to read that much-heralded passage announcing this arrival? I don't even pause to see if hands are raised. To go on.

Let me add that I (the old author of this book) don't know who is writing right now? Who is moving my fingers? Because I went to bed, stuck. *Why not just move the rest of the other book, the one with this passage in it, to right here—let it take over the rest of this book?* I told myself consolingly. *That would solve it.* But that's not what my fingers are doing. Moving by themselves, they are taking orders from somewhere else. Somewhere outside my brain. So be it Continue. I am listening.

*rbC

> To get myself into myself, these last days, to so
> shake the molecules that they stood in a new
> alignment, I had to tear down every structure
> inside myself. To make every insecurity of the
> old forms, to break up the sure knowledges of
> the molecular layers, to tell them all that they
> had no harmony any more, to throw out what
> worked, to step in and hold the magnet of my
> energy over them, to say this little universe is
> no more.

In the late 1990s, that's how I spoke to my self, using the
decade of hermitage to prepare and train "that" me to be
ready for 2022.

(Not knowing what to expect or when, she handled the
situation well, as you will too, each time you meet a much-
different self, announcing itself and then arriving no kidding.)
Here, I "dictated":

> I am wordless to say what it is that I am. Only,
> that I express it. And these former alignments
> sometimes did not feel the power to do so.

Yes, I made no bones about the fact that here I was, taking
over, although in the early 2000s, when I wrote it, it was far
from assured it would ever come to be.

Imagine if you have to assume the (supposedly extreme)
risk (worth it, because the Higher Consciousness "thinks" like
that") of giving yourself a potentially fatal illness in order
to get the adjustments in energy to "come in." To *redirect the
frequency*. At the helm, twisting the wheel dramatically. I did
and did. And it seemed no risk at all. I was sure of myself, and
the outcome, my "old" self included, for it took her by storm,
asking that she assimilate all these pieces of me she had no
idea were actually "me," that is, "her," as is the case with you,
dear reader, too, thinking of yourself multidimensionally.

In entering here, I can come in as no other than myself, that self that is known in other dimensions and that cannot come in in a lesser form. Though albeit I have been said to be in other forms.

0

It was only a prediction then. I sent out warnings:

> I could not come until it was certain that I was
> wanted and asked for and that a place would be
> held. Because I could do nothing than destroy the
> place I inhabited if it did not accommodate myself.
> Rebel against the very walls that were called me.
> Or that I found myself in. That was hypothetical.
> It was an abstraction. Naturally, it was imaginary
> if these rules that govern these energies were
> unknown. Thus, I come in, in an explanation of
> these rules and these energies—known, of course,
> spoken of and written of. Yet they did not apply
> themselves in ways left for me to do, a small space.
> Quite enough. I do not ask more. I only ask to be
> me where I am,

not declare this step an ultimatum. Only, point out and question some of the inconsistencies—glaring, opening up, therefore, this debate about what is the true scope of human energy. A good question for the Twenty-First Century.

Well, so be it. I got here. Wow. Now that I
Sign language, that the beggar used. It turned out to be—now "collapsed," these many years later—SINE LANGUAGE. A *sine.*
Ha.
—intercepting the sentence fast as lightning, snapping it in, *as if* I had consciously placed it there, which I didn't, the computer explained it to me. And you. It tells me, it is the beggar signaling to be allowed in. Of twenty-six Earth years before.

That is who it is I am or was and now have arrived. The one across the glass that had no body to set alight. Nobody. To infiltrate with pure light.

Having been given that clue to the spoken question of who I am, who is writing here, let's go on and see if the book is too inconvenienced by this intrusion. Let me guess. No. But let's see. I say no because this operator in Light surely can have the "other quanta" that are needed lined up.

I remember once at a sacred ayahuasca ceremony—yes, I participated in one twice—I felt an evolved being step into me. Well, first, I "saw" hurriedly the air rippling, as in *Star Trek* preceding where a figure reemerges into physical form; vibrating with the particles reassembling. Next thing I knew, I felt myself standing stock still, aligning around that now in-form being I knew was highly evolved, standing in me. The first thing he did was have me stretch my arms to the side, at about 28-degree angles, and silently "tell" those who wanted to know that he was here and if they wanted his assistance to go sit down at the table. I watched as several people approached the table and sat. I remained still as he "worked" on them. It's something like that now, when my fingers move, and The Man with the Light continues.

Wow! If I do say so myself. I break the silence with Wow!

Newton was forced to acknowledge that he had discovered principles that reinforced a *powerless* deity, if one at all. There was no God of Final Causes.* But something of this apparently "met the eye" these centuries hence in the dream earlier introduced—of the child Carl Jung.

The Unmoved PRIME Mover—what could better indicate (Nay, Even DEPICT) the Unmoved Mover (of Aristotle,**

_____

* To Aristotle there were four kinds of causes:
    Material
    Efficient
    Formal
    Final

** "Indeed, Aristotle considered the universe as a single organism in which each part grows and develops in its relationship to the whole and in which it has its proper place and function" (David Bohm, *Wholeness and the Implicate Order*, pp. 12–13)

of Newton) THAN—a flat elongated Third Eye of the Eastern sixth-chakra, in frozen NON-DIALOGUE on top of the head.

Nevertheless, when the picture that came into the child Jung's dream is taken down again, and we now look at it, as in walking through a gallery in "My Last Duchess," what becomes clear? Jumps out, seeing the flattened Ajna chakra motionless inside the supposed-to-be-LOTUS at the crown of the head?

That there is an impossible contrad

iction. A tension not apparent. The motion of the consciousness that looks upward and beyond the Earth has been stopped. Unqualifiedly, in a frozen stare, as if paralyzed. With what?—with disbelief, with fear, with incomprehension at the layers of crumbling that would take place in the idea world, should the *implications* of cause be carried further? Should the "nonlocal" be allowed more space in this Earth-cause explanation?

We had not ousted the original idea of geocentricity and anthropomorphicity. Only camouflaged it. Made it palatable. But in actual fact, it still dominated the deductions of the Earth. Well, I put this to you as a question. I do not assert, but only point out that it appears to be the case.

Not to the physical eye so much as to the discerning eye of beneath-the-surfaces. So, I appeal to your discernment. For answer to this.

As Leonard Shlain elaborately analyzes, "According to Einstein, light is elevated to supremacy over both space and time. Indeed, it seems instead to be the very *source* of space and time. Prosaically, we believe light rays journey light-years across vast intergalactic distances. On the contrary . . . [quoting the physicist Edward Harrison] 'Spacetime is constructed in such a way that the distance traveled by light rays is always zero'" (p. 133, Art & Physics).

This is because of its speed!

"At the speed of light the scene at the rear of the train [which imaginary people are riding in] fuses with the scene in front! The words 'ahead' and 'rear' lose their meaning and space outside the train contracts so severely that these two spatial directions are in contact with each other. Because of this queer effect, any individual looking forward sees the rear platform of the train!"

That is, outside the train. Inside, this does not appear to be so.

As for the time distortion, no mass can move at the speed of light, but "the closer we approach [it], the smaller the interval [time] between past and future is because the present is enlarging, oozing in both directions, swallowing up what was and what is yet to be in the single moment of *now*" (p. 131). Due to this relativity, Herman Minkowski named the reciprocal relationship (the complementary expansion/contraction) between space and time a fourth dimension, "the spacetime continuum" (p. 131).

Both in art (such as with Matisse, who painted the visual implications before they were speculations in science) and in science (such as in thought experiments of Einstein), the world view was bound to change.

"Both [Matisse and Einstein] in their own way assisted light to claim the crown as the rightful heir to the throne of reality"!!! (p. 186).

Light which set the outermost top speed in the universe (in the dictates of the day) and which, at such speed, annihilated the concepts of separate time and space and even of color as a thing unto itself, unaffected by speed. Yet which, in terms of itself, traveled zero distance, as space swelled to include all of undivided time. Color too was affected; that is, what color it was, at relative speeds and direction. None of which the frozen single eye, with the aura of light over it, seemed to notice. Supposing it were not just the phallic symbol that Jung finally determined, but something about The Way We See.

Without putting a map on top of a map, we proceed.

To collapse the Third Eye on top of the crown, looking frozenly above—and call the creature whose head did this "the man-eater"—might qualify for describing a stopped Evolution in Consciousness.

But it is all the evolution we've ever known.

WHAT WOULD IT IMPLY and how old would it be if whatever this stopped perspective is MOVED.

Something pervasive, giant, historical, so buried it was understood only in a dream. What is it Jung saw that needed to change??!!

The thing was that my secret nook got discovered. Where I was working in secret. Before I knew it, there were obviously new hands at work, knowing how to intercept the computer. I had to realize it, know which computer effects I did not want, but were just sheer destructiveness, and which were not weeds—but pictorial. That was it, which were pictorial? Also, which were kind? Even if something was to be cut, saying it kindly, not just rolling over the entire page with a rolling pin or a steam roller. Which consciousness was not equal to mine, even if it didn't know it? Emotional "ghettos," etc. Places that it is very dangerous to go into. We will bring up the idea that this might be true. All the "down-and-outs"—in this kind of context.

Contagious, Marlow. Are they CONTAGIOUS? And in our atmosphere? In each sneeze? Each whisking-away-of-the-hand? Each "encounter" of part of ourselves with another woman? Another man?

If nonhumans had equal rights, first of all, there would be next to nothing to eat. But then, not every fundamental law could be torn down at the same time. All the brains that depended on certain degrees of security would be tormented and a hell created right here, had it been suggested, affirmed, and required that everyone, on the spot, totally absorb multi-Level ladders (a Chain of Being) of acquired consciousness. And more to the point, there would have been virtually nothing to learn. So while this lesson was in force, these other corresponding lessons remained hidden, not drawn into focus.

It was like surrendering before there was anything to surrender to.

Next sentence. Who wants to make the next sentence???

Jung identified the man-eater with a phallic symbol, as feared by his devoutly Christian mother. He felt terror of it before she spoke.

THEREFORE

Archetypes are not only giant-size. We don't just step into three dimensions, in voids of disconnection. On the upside, these barnacle-like patterns can teach, to each and every person: TO SEE WHERE THEY

ARE.

Optical rays, Euclid said— We had studied him in school for many centuries. What we did not study was that so far as optics were concerned, he said, how we did it was—rays. All people sent them, he said, out of their eyes. Did we, now? Anyway, isn't it clear that if everything has energy, and if eyes are "turned on me," they will put energy onto me, or send it over, in any case—positive or negative? Or is that clear?

Richard Feynman, who was to make a legendary name for himself, was assigned as teaching assistant at Princeton to twenty-eight-year-old John Archibald Wheeler, whose age, at their first meeting, caught Feynman by surprise. For his doctorate, he threw himself into the topic of "least action," as applied to quantum mechanics. He got there by way of a strange theory:

> I am going to make the ... assumption that an atom never emits light except to another atom . . . it is as absurd to think of light emitted by one atom regardless of the existence of a receiving atom as it would be to think of an atom absorbing light without the existence of light to be absorbed. I propose to eliminate the idea of mere emission of light and substitute the idea of *transmission*, or a process of exchange of energy between two definite atoms . . .

So you are telling me, critics said, that I may have a rendezvous all set up with something that set out toward this destination a hundred, a million, years ago? Not many scientists were buying it. But something stuck: "As the theory developed, however, one feature gained paramount importance. It proved possible to compute particle interactions according to a principle of least action."

> The approach was precisely the shortcut that Feynman had gone out of his way to

disdain in his first theory course at MIT. For a ball arcing through the air, the principle of least action made it possible to sidestep the computation of a trajectory at successive instants of time. Instead, one made use of the knowledge that the final path would be the one that minimized action, the difference between the ball's kinetic and potential energy . . . Using the principle of least action instead of following the traditional format ["which captured a change from instant to instant"], one developed a bird's-eye perspective, envisioning a particle's path as a whole, all time seen at once. . . . The behavior of nature is determined by saying her whole space-time path has a certain character . . . The notion [of light as a wave-particle] had come far since Euclid wrote, "The rays emitted by the eye travel in a straight line."

The empty space of the physicist's imagination—the chalkboard [as it were] on which every motion, every force, every interaction played itself out—had undergone a transformation in less than a generation. A ball pursued a trajectory through the everyday space of three dimensions. The particles of Feynman's reckoning forged paths through the four-dimensional space-time so indispensable to the theory of relativity, and through even more abstract spaces whose coordinate axes stood for quantities other than distance and time. In space-time even a motionless particle followed a trajectory, a line extending from past to future. For such a path [Hermann] Minkowski coined the phrase *world-line*—"an image, so to speak, of the everlasting career of the substantial point, a curve in the world . . . The whole universe

> is seen to resolve itself into similar world-lines."
> Science-fiction writers had already begun to
> imagine the strange consequences of world-lines
> twisting back from the future into the past . . . No
> novelist was letting his fantasies roam as far as
> Wheeler was, however (pp. 120–122, *Genius*, the
> Gleick biography of Feynman).

It just says, above, that the trajectory of the whole of a line
follows the "least *action*." Not the shortest path in distance or time.

And further, this study, of Wheeler's and Feynman's, was
carried out inside questions about time—did it run backwards
and forwards?—to which Feynman replied that it ran backwards
on small scales; in the natural world, that being improbable.
However, in the particle world, not so (ibid., p. 118).

> In the end, there was an asymmetry in the
> universe of their |Wheeler's and Feynman's|
> theory—the role of ordinary retarded |past-
> to-future| fields far outweighs the advanced
> |future-to-past| fields—but that asymmetry
> does not lie in the equations. It comes about
> because of the disordered, mixed-up nature of
> the absorber.

Wait. What's that?

> It is not impossible for the ink molecules
> |diffused in a glass of water|, randomly drifting
> about, someday to reorganize themselves into a
> droplet |i.e., going backward, to form the single
> ink drop they previously were. Not impossible|.
> It is just hopelessly improbable (pp. 118–119).

For Wheeler and Feynman, their theory,

> implied a symmetry between a source and the absorber, or receiver, of the light or radiation that it emitted, even millions of light years apart, as specifically noted by a physicist, Gilbert N. Lewis, who "happened to have coined the word *photon*," because the field was no longer an independent entity [but a place where interactions occurred], the action of a particle suddenly became a quantity that made sense. (pp. 118–119).

The absorber, in our everyday world, being often us, you and me.

It makes little sense that we are "expecting" a radiation "sent out" even millions of years—a billion?—ago to be intent on reaching us, that that is its raison d'être; that we are the "cause" it radiated out into the universe in the first place, expecting we would be there, when the day came, and time, and place—to receive it! No, we can believe a lot. But this was too much, most of science said.

Imagine what that would mean if I came to Earth expecting a signal sent out a million years earlier, now "on time." Entering "time." Science would not have it.

We absorb the radiation, the light, the photon, the concept in "a symmetry between a source and the absorber, or receiver (in this instance, you and me), of the light or radiation that it emitted, even millions of light years apart"? No, not in our toolkit.

And neither are we but ill equipped to re-unite random bits of an ink molecule or pieces of a broken vase backward in time.

But can our consciousness do this? And IF IT DOES, CAN WE ABSORB IT??? Supposing we do, can the world we bring it back to?

"Twenty years later, in 1963, the problem of time having given up none of its mystery, a group of twenty-two physicists, cosmologists, mathematicians, and others sat around a table at Cornell to discuss the matter. Was time a quantity entered in the account books of their equations to mark the amount of *before* and *after*? Or was it an all-enveloping flow, carrying everything with it like a constant river? In either case, what did it mean to say *now*?" (p. 123).

Having learned about the big archetypes, THUS AND THEREFORE, must we? can we? recognize the small ones, even those so small they are unique????? (?) And those in constellations. Strings. Those that have great influence and lead to Events inside Events, prefaced on the first. Recognize (can I? you?) that my thoughts, unconsciously, might be dialoguing with someone else's, making an event more likely— that unconsciously I might be encouraging someone to do something, pouring energy into it; softly (or not) saying that I would prefer it that way. And vice versa. Only if aware of these aspects and activities of ourselves will we take responsibility for the actions we have micro-roles in. Or large, unconscious ones. We will see that when something finished in me, it might be **just starting in** someone else. If so, the energetic memory of how it finished in me might be EXERTING AN INFLUENCE THERE.

Thus, it was significant enough—but lacking all sense of the proportions it has reached—my being called to the C. G. Jung Institute in Zurich to study. In a dream. In the1980s. From there, to wind up inside Carl Jung's first remembered dream—TO FIND THAT A COLLECTIVE DREAM; that as when he dreamed of World War II images before the war (or of unfinished collective business, business of the world, and CALLED IT THAT)—so in this first dream, he was dreaming a dream for the world; for you, for me.

For everyone interested in moving out of the status quo—
which he saw frozen. Poised for change, *by the mere fact of being
perceived*. Humanity—in its strength—put its unconscious
wisdom into the child's head, which was able to hold it, bring
it back from sleep, *to remember the dream*.

Humanity knew, even then, where it was. It could find itself
relative to a higher consciousness, gauging just what amount
of information it would take to go one step further. To shake
loose of this position. To take a step into the future. In this
terminology, that meant a change of position, a shift of angle,
a dropping-away of the collective larger pattern. Not the
small patterns inside the giant overarching preconceptions,
presumptions, ABCs of our life. THE pattern itself.

So, the child Jung dreamed WHERE THE EARTH WAS.
Dreamed humanity's unconscious consciousness.

Now, this consciousness—so alert it could depict itself
this clearly—had other points of contact. It had *contact points
within itself*, points where the ability to diagram the Earth
relationship to Consciousness was present.

Meanwhile, then, like a slow ship of state moving into re-
election situation, this old-new consciousness—*this heritage of
the open mind*—prepared a stunning blow. It prepared to seed
the Earth with its own memory. To blast below the structure
of the Earth, to the very heart of its ancient knowledge. It
prepared to revive the dead Earth, it prepared a new season
on the Earth, it prepared to Re-Birth the entire Earth. It was
much simpler than it might sound, following, as it did, from
everything above.

There is a fundamental Planck *temperature*,
which is likely to be the hottest anything
can get. Compared with it, everything in our
experience, even the interiors of stars, is barely
above absolute zero. This means that, in terms
of fundamental things, the universe we observe
is frozen. We begin to get the feeling that we

know as much about nature and its potential phenomena as a penguin knows of the effects of forest fire, or of nuclear fusion. This is not just an analogy—it is our real situation. We know that all materials melt when raised to a high enough temperature. If a region of the world were raised to the Planck temperature, the very structure of the geometry of space would melt. The only hope we have of experiencing such an event is by peering into our past, for what is usually called the big bang is, in fundamental terms, the big freeze . . . To understand space and time in their natural terms, we have to imagine what was there before everything around us froze. (p. 63, *Three Roads to Quantum Gravity*)

Look! Just as he said!—the vision mechanism of the "man-eater" (which he saw) is a Frozen Eye. Well, IT DIDN'T HAVE TO BE THAT WAY.

Why? Because the child saw the strange-headed creature, with the frozen single eye, staring overhead, as something negative. The "the man-eater."

Starting with a promise that seemingly could not be fulfilled, that fragment of humor and outrage thrust into the commentary, we wind up in being taken at our word. It was the universe's word that was at stake, its promise to all those standing inside the energy of the Promise. That their commitment would not go to waste. The promise of their buildups—inside what there was no way to see. For it had not happened. There was no assurance it would.*

---

*Each time we pause to contemplate our lives and wonder in amazement at the patterns that are emerging, stunned at how unconscious we are and how much we do not know; each time we allow ourselves to feel our emotions to their fullest, to think our thoughts all the way through to their fullest clarity; each time we take the risk of expressing ourselves honestly and deeply, the Trickster breathes deeply and smiles and transforms into the Willing Sacrifice" (p. 260, Jeremy Taylor).

If at each risk, instead of walking away, if they poured in more energy, made the stakes of investment as high as could be borne, these carriers of our inheritance, acting on orders and requests unconsciously sent out by the people of the Earth, demonstrated the underlying process of cause/effect as it is always carried forth. Carried forth even inside the convictions that ruled it out, denied, antimatter-related to it. And temporarily had often in the past. But "temporarily" passed into collective conviction.

Strategically, day by day, in the unknown, the Ante was being UPPED. Not downed, we remind you. It was clearly, as will become pronouncedly clear, being upped.

The movement of the Earth into its new consciousness

continued, grew, remained. Here to

stay.

Moving out of the practice of identifying with what we see in the external world and not with the see-r: the thought processes inside the brain—the brainwaves—that influence the picture. The thought that it is outside makes and pushes it outside. Because we do not identify it as interacting with what we think before we saw it or at the time. The vision of the parade tra

nsported me, not because the reality of 1
do with something important for me to
jectory orbits to that present instant.) N
AS NOT THERE. The only way it co
nsPORTED, docking at harbors that DI
airports—like the planes that existed in
y did here—TRANSPORTED by a proces
) NOT, IN GENERAL, KNOW. YET

nsported me, not because the reality of the physical parade had to do with something important for me to know. (Its own chaotic trajectory orbits to that present instant.) No. What was important WAS NOT THERE. The only way it could be was in symbol, transported, docking at harbors that DID NOT EXIST, landing at airports—like the airplanes that existed in Leonardo's mind before they did here—TRANSPORTED by a process of communication WE DO NOT, IN GENERAL, KNOW. YET WE PRACTICE ALL

THE SAME.

enying that we do. LIVING IN A STATE OF

THE SAME. While d
DENIAL. I abdicate

THE SAME. While denying that we do. Living in a state of DENIAL. I abdicate this state. Make my place in that other estate—the heritage of humanity; the one side by side with, penetrating, and influencing, the accepted reality and worldview.

Hosannas and Cheers

Archetypes, said Jung, with Wolfgang Pauli, bridged or mediated between matter and psyche. A synchronicity, in which an action carried forth a kinetic message, parallel to a physical representation that was *somewhere else* through an action that was unvoiced—the voiceless container sent acknowledgment to some unconscious area, which knew what it viewed. Now, this being an ingenious expression of what we are, organisms, a life form, or soul, which—on the one hand—does not routinely supposedly use psychic powers, such as to telescope a vision, a statement, into the head of another, as in dying. Nor through its own self (or aspects of self). Yet here, gives the emissary-commission *to a thought, which goes out and finds its equivalent, its likeness.* So how?

Let's go on. And find out. For I could look back and see that sporadically this format was exactly the one I had been in or communicated to through. Or had myself, in some capacity unconscious to me, communicated to myself with, such as even—to start there, as we did—in the piano *contour*; the shape of that event—as *not finishing*—passing through the whole gamut of options of how to play the piece (or some of the variants), before standing up again, at The End, in the right sequence. Was this catching "the verbal on the fly," spelled out in minutiae so there could be no mistake, that it did all the time?

As synchronicity was the voice of psyche, then the fact that sound, as vibration, predated almost everything, sending impulses that caused creations to occur—as waves passed through prestar materials, —the ancient nonspoken "sound" "voice" of psyche into matter was something we'd do well to listen to. Or at least, it would be exciting to.

So these pieces of kinetic, symbolic action (such as the beggar at the window, mouthing a request—miming—in a start-to-finish wavy line; or the parade, paralleling simultaneously—clairvoyantly?—the end of a life), were they in symmetry to the essence, concretized, "localized" presence of a thing—whose meaning might be in AN ACTION, demonstrating, even, that "principle of least action, killing two birds with one stone? A kind of teleported meaning, hiding in an action, as it might have in a materialized object, or transporting itself to *where there was something to communicate*. Or taking advantage of an action under way, on the scene, in location.

½ mv², wrote Jung, citing the basic mathematical formula for kinetic energy.

What?

I looked again.

It was accurate, scientifically known!

Kinetic energy had its very own formula. KE: one half of mass times velocity²!!!!

The mathematical formula only by analogy related to psychic energy. Nevertheless, he added, the analogy between the two "is itself an older, intuitive idea from which the concept of physical energy originally developed," a primitive "extraordinarily potent" concept, related to the modern "libido"; not to forget, he goes on, that the "energetic aspect" of psyche neither "embraces [n]or explains the whole of psyche" (p. 103, On *the Nature of* Psyche, from Basic Writings).

And again comes the tricky question of whether there is something more in the sunlight. Such as whether it is at all implicated in the question of where information comes from—does light carry information in it, or is it only there, in electronics, after we, important and brilliant that we are, put it there? (Not that we aren't important and brilliant.)

Cutting the cord from these universal processes does not do, NOT WHEN WE ARE BEING BORN INTO A NEW CONSCIOUSNESS THAT GOES BACK TO ITS ORIGINS—TO THEN STEP FORTH, INDEPENDENT ONCE AGAIN.*

---

* If the universe were expanding, AND NOT THE RANGE OF LIGHT WE SEE IN, would we be getting hopelessly myopic. Less and less relative to what we saw? Except we solved that right off. Before learning that the universe expanded, we invented objects that could see it better for us. So that by the time we found out, we had already the work behind us that allowed us to keep up.

In the early days of lunettes (eyeglasses), it would have been hopeless to extend length of life, because everyone would have been blind. So first came *lunettes*, and then lengthened lifetime. But to get back to the subject: in the early days of glasses, there was a prevailing distrust of mechanical things; even to look through the glass was suspect, as it changed the size of what was seen. But just suppose, for we like suppositions— Suppose that the world that expanded also, without any announcement, expanded the realm of visible light, or of things visible. It would be one of those other hard-and-fast truths that bent with the time, or stepped back and let us see behind it. So that we would see that there were many ranges of creation, as we already knew, and perhaps some Prometheus would show us the further ranges, if only just a glimpse. So, we put this into the can of things that seemed possible to bait our subject further with. For it could be true. Most earnestly. We could fast be becoming, if the universe was expanding, like all the shut-eyed inhabitants of various "corners" of the Earth who discovered and recorded inABILITIES to see what they had "never heard of." Oh, no, the inhabitants shouted. "NOT US." I heard that shout, you see. AND RUSHED FORTH.

Now, the commonplace plant works in roughly the same range of light that is visible to us; i.e., where we stop seeing, they stop integrating the frequency (of sunlight) into their photosynthesis procedure.*

"Either by eating plants or eating animals which ate plants [such as the chlorophyll in grass], man acquires this solar energy, which is then made available to power his brain and muscles and to keep him warm."

---

*You can never make a statement and rest comfortable, sure it will still be true—or scientifically true—at the time of publication of a book. Thus, a new study in 2018 at the University of Georgia says humans do see ultraviolet light, at least young ones, 100 percent of those tested.

In an entirely straightforward text, Ford speaks of "stored chemical energy in plants," and thus, "the flow of energy from sun to earth to man . . . illustrates both the variety [of its manifestations] and the conservation of energy" (p. 27, in Ferris, ed.). Eating plants means having first access to this energy traveling from the solar light, "the energy content of the photons," these "bundles of electromagnetic energy" that is involved in photosynthesis; that is, after the plants transformed it—suitably, for us. What meaning for consciousness might it have whether to draw the solar energy from the plants (which are not meat-eaters, or man-eaters), or by way of animals (which are); is that different??? For one thing, there is no surrounding gestalt in which something died (because we do not count the "death" of the sun ray), when a plant "eats" and passes on the solar energy.

CHAPTER 8

Refuting Ortega y Gasset

"I am myself and my circumstances."

NO—

shot back Milton Klonsky—

Let all the colors in the world change, they blind us to the fact that "The Dome remains the same."

How to wrap this all up when so many threads seemed entirely timely, AND WERE DRAWING TOGETHER MORE AND MORE?

Well, this was going to take a major reorientation

That is, if I figured out the posthumous message I was trying to decipher, and thus deliver intact, with meaning, flavor, and actual direction and recommendation, whereby *this time* the Dome did *not* remain the same.

Which was what had been asked for, back then. And all along, to boot. Once the statement, for my perusal, had been made. Up there in the "eyrie," or eagle's nest, where I first heard it, in New York City on the ninth floor in an apartment occupied by Milton Klonsky, whose many adages, left unexplained and furled, are now being reopened.

What was the book of this life, the one unwritten yet spoken, that I had striven to get portions of down in print, felt it left in my hands??? What did it say? deeper and deeper into the issues of the times, when looked at with a more unflinching, sturdy eye:

> [T]o the devoutly rational and/or rationally devout [Sir Isaac] Newton himself, for whom both the Word and the Work [Bible and Creation] reflected the Supreme Intelligence, faith as well as reason joined in one hallelujah of an ergo: a divine Plan in nature meant that there was an equally divine Plot in history. It was a Plot, moreover, discerned in broad outline by the prophets, that subsumed all other sub-, side-, cross-, or counterplots, a Plot of plots, unfolding the destiny of mankind *in saecula saeculorum* as a religious drama with a beginning, a middle, and an eschatological cherry at The End. (p. 129, *Art & Life*)

Skipping to the last page of this essay:

> "The only difference between a shaman and an epileptic," declares Mircea Eliade [a great

difference indeed] "is that the latter cannot deliberately enter into trance." And [Eliade] points to the extreme cold of Arctic regions, the long nights and glacial solitude, the lack of fats and vitamins in the diet, and the sense of cosmic oppression felt by the inhabitants as "giving rise either to mental illness (Arctic hysteria) or to shamanic trance." Yet that trance perhaps may lie at the bottom of the Dream [of humanity] and at the beginning of the Plot [that Newton had had pronounced belief in].

For it was under similar climactic conditions], when the Earth was alive and four great Ice Age trolls—Gunz, Mindel, Russ, and Würm— stalked up and down the Pleistocene, that the unkillable fire-eyed elves, who are Everyman, first emerged gripping their flint-axe pheons, hiding out in caves and in the bosky interstices of glacial valleys, and so survived from day to day and from millennium to millennium until the present. The worst plots, thought Aristotle, are the episodic, except those that go round in a circle. After all our hypothetical leaps and bounds in pursuit of the metaphorical Flea—*there it is!*—perhaps that's what it was foreordained to come to in The End:

MAN like a Flea shall

jump from star to

(pp. 187–188, Milton Klonsky, *Art & Life: A Menippean Paean to the Flea; or, Did Dostoevsky Kill Trotsky?*).

This would do. Enough to sleep on, digest, ruminate on, bring forth, as an added driving fuel (of which there were already several) to get us through the rest of this book.

And here we are, in that connecting link into where the Earth is anchored and what moorings are being reattached, refocused, redirected, in our journeys into the days, years, millennia, ahead. Right now.

Back in a snatch.

CHAPTER NINE

This time, 2002

*T*his time, 2002, a lot was different.

The ceiling wasn't higher—in fact, felt lower. Fallen some notches. Why?

It seemed that is, with events taking over—the prospect of the Iraq War looming, like a vast horizontal animal, crawling over the earth, or a gray typhoon—there was an organic movement, but on the animal level.

"Emergency" occupying so much of global energy, the usual powerlessness of mass consciousness was replaced by a kind of hypnotism before the scope, speed, life-and-death scale of the events, and beside that there were few single irresistible, overriding voices raised up powerfully inspiring the planet with wisdom—the power to put a halt to all deception "of the people," to see though the deceptions on the world scene and place them in a context that was viable, WITHOUT WAR.

Survival/fear were the energies sent out over the earth, through the news. And these reports had utter urgency.

There were so many entry points for problems. Mass consciousness was globalized, and it was impotent regarding truth as a transparent fact. But it was not impotent in feeling "SOMETHING IS WRONG."

So it acted, but blindly, sure that something was out of sync with truth. Nothing could penetrate, when marching with the shield of "fear," whoever did.

Merely to project a hypothetical, possible, negative event down a not-yet-here road in the future was possibly to give that very route momentum! It was a ghastly situation.

The eye put together pieces, to get a unified object and view. Vision was always by composite. We had to stop "filling in the blanks" with automatic back-looking assumptions about how to respond. Understand that the DOME OF THE EARTH WAS BEING LIFTED. Trying to be.

The consultation point had been preempted by groups who could not see beyond the scenes on the screen..

Where was this leading?

So. I thought that I was speaking like an extremist. But like always, I looked inside. HOW DID IT FEEL? It felt LIKE THIS.

I stopped. I waited for more insight. SOME CAME.

People were scared.

AND WELL THEY SHOULD BE.

※

So I thought that if I started like this, it would certainly get me somewhere. By staring at the void, the emptiness from solution, or the turning away from solution, the confrontational atmosphere—by not yielding to the fear, neither to the cut-off level where the Earth consciousness was now residing. Surely the Earth could not survive in such a consciousness.

That was one thing dead-sure.

But I suddenly remembered the meditation that opened this present volume. It had spoken entirely of solutions. Where were those solutions?

INSIDE HUMANS.

"No longer could exploration be *outside only. Here, in the human energy, located inside the memory banks and experiential reasonings and answers dormant in individuals, and the collective, were the hope of tomorrow. Buried, waiting CREATION. Buried in the creative energies themselves!!. . ."*

We were a secret resource, containers of the raw material of thought, the mechanism to free us the Earth counted on: holders of the *information capacity* to solve its/our problems.

At the boundary of the All, where a new center was waiting to be forged, a call was going out. ALL was calling, calling ALL Of humanity, any who felt THE CALL. Nameless and without a mantle of authority even, just standing for "US ALL."

All was informing individual listeners that the dome of the Earth had fallen below the Point of The All. And the Earth would rise or fall—breathe or feel claustrophobic—according to whether or not we discovered, isolated put under a microscope like all the other things we had put there, and so discovered not just the ability to break things apart, master the process of collision and split—but beyond that, re-creation.

For on the subatomic level, what did they lead to? Death (which in consciousness would be symbolic). But at the same time, for things happened so quickly on subatomic levels, relative to us, to Higher Unity. Re-creation, where light met light and a new light emerged. A transfiguration, a resurrection even, if you will. To Inserting Consciousness into Collisions! That was the other side of the coin!

We had the urgent need to wrest a new vision from what was going on. To take the mantle of the human race, the species, and find where its good points lay. With the Dome fallen, the top level of consciousness—the top frequencies of the planet—accessible through the open Dome, let us not, the bulk of humanity, be distancing ourselves from them.

How could a planet survive IF ITS TOP FREQUENCIES, the inspiration that had drawn it to its mercurial solutions, its ingenious inventions—if that level of mind, of spirit, retreated, and was not on speaking terms with it? If its voices, at the level it would take now, on the planet were stilled, and only War and dissension took over the throat of the planet?

And where were the pure chimes of the tingle of peace and joy? There had to be this AT THE TOP, but it had retreated. And where? And why?

As if the sound of peace had been killed from the planet. For otherwise, wouldn't it be speaking out? Gradually, gaining speed. And if not accessible in the range of vision of all the leaders, if up there in the ultraviolet rays (instead leaving the ultraVIOLENT DOWN HERE), what were we to do, to find those now ultraviolet teachings, insights, sudden wisdoms and solutions That would save, by including us all.

I retreated. I had to think how to make my way back up to the "higher wisdom," the higher frequencies, without abandoning the Earth, which, it appeared to me, was looking for these frequencies. And could not see them in the physical sites.

So, what kind of gauntlet was it for the Earth? And who suddenly pulled the plug, or, as it were, pushed the "red button"—for on one level, pushing the red button only meant sending up THE ARCHETYPE OF WAR. Of annihilation. Hoping, planning, intending, that the EARTH CHOOSE NOT TO ANSWER THE CALL. To recognize and

NOT ANSWER THE CALL.

The Earth was being challenged to learn how to

NOT ANSWER THE CALL.

Not be fooled by rhetoric and words as before. Not feel impotent, inside the mass consciousness, as the mass consciousness had every right to. Not be left with an uneducated, untransformed ego, AT THIS POINT, not be left "not knowing what they do." All this had to be rectified, was part of the new archetype amassing. But behind the scenes, below visibility level. For none of us here, TILL NOW, had learned how to see into THE ULTRAVIOLET SPHERE.

We had not learned to detect the rays of light, the way plants do, read the registers without any mechanical instruments. Know LIGHT inside and out. Bask and relish inside atmosphere itself, the mere environment. We were about to LEARN HOW.

I was reminded that in Zurich, the Initiator had told me of an archetype of The End of the World. Get it folks, *a symbolic end*. The true end being of The Old Consciousness. We, in our all-too-often habit of seeing the physical dimension and no further, had to get the point, or at least act as if we did, that a mentality was at war, at stake (not physical armies), we might act out the archetype in.

Was the other polarization merely mirrors, sometimes faulty—or rather, all faulty, but some more than most—in fact, exact opposites of this true archetype. Life or Death. Survival or not. DEATH OF THE OLD CONSCIOUSNESS, DEATH OF THE OLD EARTH. BUT—let it not be physical.

Physically focused consciousness was going to have to learn to not think it was up to every challenge. IT WAS NOT. Hopefully, we were to gain immense foresight-wisdom.

The tuning fork of the planet had been forming alignments of hindsight; of vision that biased what it saw—interjecting words and interpretations into the pieces of fact, to stitch them together, preconditioned by what it already knew or at least could feel secure in, pull out "for example." But the method of seeing was shifting. How else could one see in the present but by giving up—down the road, eventually—HINDSIGHT, especially if the stakes were the preservation of the planet?

Let the earth glow in this example of transformation and transfiguration. A model of how a planetary consciousness underwent the change from physically based interpretation to the personally responsible scale, where each individual realized the importance of processing its personally particular knowledge. *From the angle it received it in*. The unique angle of one person's position, which was not to be jumped out of lightly, in speaking—for just as in atomic shells, that position cannot be held by another.

Too much of the planetary consciousness was in latent energy, and therefore spoken for by a presuming visible person, who did not have those particular facts but absconded with the energy of the person with the unprocessed facts—picking it up and "Filling in the Blanks."

As a blank to start with, the fall of Atlantis, as told by Plato—or not by Plato, stopped in mid-air, mid-sentence (whether never written or lost), as if feeling it unnecessary in that time period, reserved for later relevance, when the wheels of karma or repetition spiraled round, AND THERE WE WERE AGAIN. In that time of—this time—a playout of the archetype of the Death of the Old Earth.

OR—magnificent thrusting upward of the ceiling of the Earth vault, its Reality Threshold, so that we could see in the open air of the universe beyond. The ideas that we could process *together* by letting go the hold of the old regressive ideas, the assumptions about "What Being Human Was." The expectation of battles between War and Peace, like two great Greek gods in battle. And saw what reconfigurations the planet might have if it thought differently. Let go the certainty of these old archetypes as the only possible ones here. AND WAITED WITH BATED BREATH TO SEE what might come next.

For the way things stood now, it was considered reasonable, normal, entirely realistic to assume humans, in all the rawness and lack of compassion, WERE THE PEAK POINT OF THE SPECIES.

But no, some higher consciousness threshold was offered, as it were, because between the two choices of continuing in the old direction and resuming as a planet, moving in conscious pride of unity, then there was only one vote. One answer the planet would give if even a few voices began to hold up such a tuning fork. People were parroting words like "enough is enough," put into the wrong contexts, holding out false hope.

So, a new state prepared its entry, the state the Earth had built up to, by speaking of it so often, in so many parts of the globe, and planting it firmly into the hearts of the inhabitants, almost to a one.

But then, in more practical language, say that it had become possible for the reasoning brain to imagine it as logical. Even science had contributed. One could, in a whisper, add that science had contributed resoundingly!!!—standing first of all in this matter, as it also led the way in smashing the atom.

Science had made the tenets of higher consciousness, if one thought about it from certain angles, reasonable. Realistic. And if one went on in certain lines of thinking, more or less proved.

I was eager to see how the next part would unfold, just as I tried to track it down. The Positive. The planetary LIGHT. Where was that Light now, when standing in a unifying position? Was it outside the window? Did I, like each person in their own position, have to see it—*where no one else did*? And respond by giving it material? Was Light looking for matter to make events with, to write on blank pages with??? Was this the page we were turning???

Meanwhile, on the home front, I was suffering from a lowering of vibration; or, to put it differently, lack of high frequency readily available in the environment.

215

I felt like a heretic at times, an outcast. Because always protesting that the solution wasn't being sought for in the high frequencies. But then, in some quarters, this was being widely said. Right here. Yes, definitely. How to "connect" so that the electricity was readily available, the high frequency pushing through the barriers. The cap, the Dome. YES.

Did people know about the possibility of suffocation from LOW or lowered VIBRATION?

Why, yes.

Exactly.

Lowered, producing distortion of interpretation, emotion,

the prediction that if there was no transition, there would be Debauchery.

Marching into that now.

Already partway THRU'

And what to *open the sea*???

A vibration would

A collective vibration, that knocked through the individual ones, on various pitches and at various tones, and made a sustainable NEW MASS VIBRATION FOR THE EARTH because—

there was NO OTHER WAY THRU'

No old solution would do.

There were too many partially right solutions

But let all of humanity in on it. Let them notice how to

include them too—
   as well-meaning people saw one possible future, one
straight line, or several allied ones.

AND DID NOT SEE
PERIPHERALLY.
But the Earth itself had peripheral vision.
It had people on
ALL SIDES OF EVERY QUESTION NOW!!!!!!!!!

This was it—
our entry into
the twenty-first century
WIS-
DOM

DOM-
INGO*
flamingo

---

* *domingo*: Sunday (Sp)

Sun-
dés
dice
But this theme is up ahead.
approaching.

Not only was there now, on the Earth, peripheral vision,
but coming in at its side,
as opposites met,
VISCERAL
VISION

I had finally figured out, for one starts with oneself,
the purpose of the sign most extravagantly in my astrology,
Mars-Neptune, at a strength to make it dominate my life.
Mars-Neptune WAR/PEACE

Was it in the center of the planetary evolution now
as a by-product to
RESTORE THAT BALANCE
It figured.

Backtracking and forward tracking, I kept doggedly trying
to find out where all the clues in the collective unconscious
that had passed my way, and that I had stopped for, attracted
as if an Alchemist beating them into gold,

WERE TELLING US THIS EARTH WAS SECRETLY AND
NOW FASTLY, with great effectiveness and loud blasts, and
not a few tooted horns

MOVING TO.*

---

* I told myself that John Milton was born on "Bread Street," as if it had some
significance. Gave it emphasis. I said, now listen everyone sit up and take
notice. Not that they did, of course. Not one single person, in the billions
even, in the present Earth said that this had meaning. At least, so far as we
knew. And we did not know everything, by ANY MEANS or even "every." So,
silence all around, we kept going. After all, this had led to Jung's cavelike
"Underground" with the "throne." Where else was it leading????

"The universe as a whole is in a pure state," Seth Lloyd said. "But individual pieces of it, *because they are entangled with the rest of the universe*, are in mixtures. (emphasis added)

> Lloyd spent several years studying the evolution of particles in terms of shuffling 1s and 0s. He found that as the particles became increasingly entangled [their information intertwined], with one another, the information that originally described them [who you are, who I am, for instance] (a 1" for clockwise spin and a 0" for counterclockwise, for example) would shift to describe the system of entangled particles as a whole.

What this means? In layman's terms, please.

> It was as though the particles [the particles inside you and me, for instance] gradually lost their individual autonomy and became pawns of the collective state.

Yes, pawns.

> Eventually, the correlations contained all the information, and the individual particles contained none. . . What's really going on is things are becoming more correlated with each other," Lloyd recalls realizing. "The arrow of time [that goes in one direction only in 3-D] "is an arrow of increasing correlation."
> The idea, presented in his 1988 doctoral thesis, fell on deaf ears . . . "I was damn close to driving a taxi cab," Lloyd said.
> According to the scientists, our ability to remember the past but not the future, another

historically confounding manifestation of time's arrow, can also be understood as a buildup of correlations between interacting particles. When you read a message on a piece of paper, your brain becomes correlated with it through the photons that reach your eye!!!!! [emphasis added] Only from that moment on will you be capable of remembering what the message said. As Lloyd put it, "The present can be defined by the process of becoming correlated with our surroundings."

The backdrop for the steady growth of entanglement throughout the universe is, of course, time itself. [Natalie Wolchover "Time's Arrow Traced to Quantum Source"]

So, I merge with my surroundings. I am myself and my circumstances???

This says that information does not stay fixed in a head when it interacts with a surrounding setting. No, it begins to seep down into the setting and intermingle.

The lightning bolt of individual knowledge begins to lose strength, dwindle, dilute, disappear into "the Whole." Or: the setting. Therefore, an artist such as Faulkner keeps his mouth shut, as he did during hunts. The other hunters talked around the campfire. He remained in a "wall of silence." Why? Well, he was *not intermingling, a hunter friend of his told me, in a firsthand account Not sinking down into the mass consciousness, not falling into the pit of commonality. As Milton Klonsky told me of a particular situation, "You sink to the lowest common denominator." Oh no. Oh yes. That's how individual entanglement works vis-à-vis entanglement, entropy.*

CAVES, WALLS, AND
BEGGED QUESTIONS

I talked to an archeologue. The Romanian cave is not a cave, he said.

What? How could the cave not be a cave?

Well, it was a monastery in the nineteenth century, and probably had various "reincarnations" in different uses. It was manmade. Humans put huge crystals in the walls, now stolen (used in ceremonies); it had two drawings in interior wall chambers. In this and other ways, it deserved (I thought) to be looked at in this trail, to see where it might have come from and what ancient practices it taught.

Jung saw a painting on a wall in Ravenna!!! WAS IT THERE???? HE saw it, as did his companion. When he later told a friend traveling to the same spot to look at it, IT WAS NOT THERE. What called forth this *invisible-the-moment-before* wall tapestry?

In the Baptisery of the Orthodox in Ravenna, he wrote, where "I remembered having seen [it] on my first visit, there were now four great mosaic frescoes of incredible beauty which, it seemed, I had entirely forgotten." This took place in the Baptistery, near the tomb of Galla Placidia, under a "mild blue light" whose apparent lack of source did not seem important.

EXACTLY WHERE DOES THIS SAY WE ARE?? ???

The carving on the cave wall in Făgăraş, Romania—suppose I had never seen it (or it had never been there). No matter. Apparently, I was following an unconscious Jungian Archetype of Individuation. I know this because—for the very early, skeletal draft conclusion of *Love in Transition*, volumes I/II—at the End finally came the discovery of—a painter in a cave. Internally. Unknown to me, because I had not yet read Jung, it harked to the looming presence of my animus, a part of me, in fact, here now. Begging for my attention, he was.

I had sensed the denouement—the epiphany where a man was reached inside the female protagonist (me), waiting to draw me to *where he could be seen*. A painter, in contact with my visual hemisphere, with paintings on walls like the one hidden deep within the cave.

Somehow communicating with me, the fact that some question had been turned aside from. When? How long ago? Or was it a light thing then, and only called into real urgency now? Then perhaps, it had been appropriate. But not now. Then, perhaps, it had even been a noble sacrifice. Had it? But in this script, its moment had "arrived."

Years later, the physical Romanian cave had a face on its inner wall, deep inside in darkness. Jung had spoken in terms of an Underground Christ, a Christ Archetype.

But is this not the *beggar on the other side of the window*.

There is, however, a real cave, somewhere. And a real face. That fact, I seem to recognize and/or remember. I no longer exactly know in what time frame "remember" is.

Therefore, this is clearly the archetype of the universal Inner Christ (or Inner Light, higher consciousness, the Self, for the term transforms and reconfigures as the writing continues, even if initially waiting to be transformed as I transform), which I said it was all the time.

BUT LOOK HOW IT PROVED ITSELF. It is everywhere, the conclusion. Once it is

somewhere, suddenly look
how IT IS EVERYWHERE.

Jung noted: "I was vexed to find my memory so unreliable." The four mosaics which Jung and his companion "saw" were the baptism in the Jordan; the passage through the Red Sea; a third "soon faded from memory." And "most impressive of all": Peter being helped by Jesus Christ when he was sinking in the water. "We stopped in front of this mosaic for at least twenty minutes and discussed the original ritual of baptism, especially the curious archaic conception of it as an initiation connected with real peril of death." (p. 315)

Jung decided, when informed later that it had been a "hallucination," the vision was "a momentary new creation by the unconscious, arising out of his thoughts about archetypal initiation." Calling it "among the most curious events of my life," saying it lacked explanation, he described a layered attraction of his anima to the "vision," which convincingly displayed itself on the wall. He said: "The anima of a man has a strongly historical character. As a personification of the unconscious she goes back into prehistory, and embodies the contents of the past." (pp. 316–317)

> In the course of my confrontation with the anima I had actually had a brush with those perils which I saw represented in the mosaics. I had come close to drowning. The same thing happened to me as to Peter, who cried for help and was rescued by Jesus. What had been the fate of Pharaoh's army could have been mine. Like Peter and like Naaman [cleansed of leprosy in the Jordan], I came away unscathed, and the integration of the unconscious contents made an essential contribution to the completion of my personality.
>
> What happens within oneself when one integrates previously unconscious contents with the consciousness is something which can scarcely be described in words. (p. 317)

All across the Earth the integrations are going on. As here, they can be devastatingly original, unbelievable. It is not the time of marching joylessly and laxly into a great new age but of justifying the claim of the Earth to have a right to march forth *into the universe.*

Possibly it was the unconscious that was conscious—to a large degree—and perhaps, if so, it is some tribute here to the survival of that idea of Jung's, in reverse, too late to explain or write about, that comes through nonetheless, like an after-striking-the-ball vibration. Or perhaps this is some Ravenna of my own, stacked on top of the imaginary frescoes, to add then these frescoes, and someone else will stand on them with some closing words.

So, while someone walks through, with a slingblade, me, and it is the slingblade normally for Conclusions, we will assume we know nothing about it, and see where it leads.

Many "thens" in the past there was no question of choices for me so radical as to be "from" another entire level of consciousness, or "universe"—measured in terms of distance from the choices previously in place. But there was a sparsity of world leaders speaking up, visionaries of these proportionate speeches and themes. Of others, but not these.

And then our very unconscious took that role. It would speak up loud and clear for us.

So the fact that I was under bombing (in not taking to the printer the text as completed in December 1999) was, rather than invasive and destroying IF I COULD INTEGRATE THE FEROCIOUS SERIOUSNESS, not to unbalance the positive energy but to underscore that it was reenforced in mighty armies, for the Earth to walk through its initiation at the End of This Century and One Quarter Almost of the Now-Next. What that was, we had, on some scales, really not been told. What I was experiencing was a scale I knew nothing of. Of balancing the ages, by reading our past in a different way.

What I called the "bombed" material, wiped into near-unreadability in the printouts (a few samples inserted but removed), was not telling me to give up. It was saying that it was here to help. How? The rest, we will see, having this thread too—to add now, to our many time schemes.

Rather than in visions, I was here in some dimension where the page took the place of the outer world. The "page," containing ideas. That dimension. Yes, I guess. Everyone, take heed. That dimension, as source.

Stan Gooch, *The Double Helix of the Mind: The Secrets of Mental Evolution and Advance*, p. 59:

> Very often, both in common speech and psychological theory we refer to the unconscious mind as being "below." We speak of the *sub*-conscious, within us, of the *under*world, of calling up or *raising* a devil, of sinking into unconsciousness, of falling asleep, conversely of surfacing to consciousness. We sink into a reverie or a depression. Most tales of horror and the supernatural involve a descent— into cellars, pits, caves or whatever. All these metaphors and allusions are unequivocal and universal, and they are well catered for by the concept of the cerebellum (that is, of cerebellar consciousness), which is *literally* situated below the cerebrum and below normal consciousness. [Robert] Ornstein's views [involving only two brain hemispheres, right and left] cannot accommodate these metaphors. For nowhere do we find any allusion to the unconscious being *to one side* of consciousness, except in the sense that the left hand is often associated with the occult. But a better explanation of that association, I suggest, is provided by the fact that the cerebellum [with its own two hemispheres, making a total of four in the human brain] itself is left-handed so far as the cerebrum [right and left hemispheres] is concerned.

227

If you ask Christof Koch, Ph.D., Chief Scientist and President of the Allen Institute for Brain Science, how close we are to understanding our own brains, he scoffs.

"We don't even understand the brain of a worm," Koch said.[14]

CREATIVITY:
BACK TO THE POINT
THE ONE-POINTED FOCUS

Wrinkles in Time, p. 36:

One reason Einstein initially rejected this implication [that the universe is either contracting or expanding—not static, in a "constant state"] of his general relativity theory was that, if the universe is currently expanding, then long ago it must have started from a single point. All space and time would have been bound up in that "point," an infinitely dense, infinitely small "singularity." Hence it would be impossible to calculate what happened "before" the singularity, as any calculations would yield nonsensical results. The singularity would be an ultimate barrier to human knowledge, and this struck Einstein as absurd.

⁂

If we look at the stars and their cousins in the distant galaxies, they appear to rotate overhead—once every twenty-four hours. However, compared to the plane of the Solar System, the observed rotation of the galaxies is less than one second of arc per century. If we go to the Earth's poles and hang a pendulum on a long cord and let it swing freely, then the plane of its swinging stays fixed relative to the distant galaxies rather than rotating with the Earth. In other words, its course of natural motion is aligned with the distant stars . . . (p. 39, Smoot).

Einstein detested [Willem] de Sitter's model ["in which a universe without matter would *expand*"] because it contained no matter. How could space make sense without matter? Matter *defined* space. (p. 40).

231

Of course, regarding a nonstatic universe, de Sitter WAS RIGHT.

Expansion FROM A POINT, a single point. The possibility OF EXPANSION from within. Into the expanding exterior. What was within was already *in potentia*:
Poe-
Tent

But few know of his [E. A. Poe's] serious interest in science, especially astronomy, and his fascination with the French astronomer Pierre-Simon de Laplace's nebular hypothesis, according to which the Solar System evolved from a primordial cloud of dust and gas . . .

According to Poe, [what is called Henrich] Olbers's paradox [that the universe was infinite, in spite of the fact that the night sky was dark, which is counterintuitive] is resolved because "[The] distance of the invisible background [is] so immense that no ray from it has yet been able to reach us at all." What Poe had stumbled upon was the fact that the universe is not infinitely old, but had a beginning in time (a point we now regard as the big bang). In fact, the universe is so young that light from the more distant stars is still speeding toward us but hasn't yet reached us. (p. 28)

✺

FAULKNER and the Concentration "topic"

The entry into the unconscious came through differently in William Faulkner—than as described to us by Marcel Proust, contained in the smell of a cake, the *madeleine*. Faulkner told us how a photograph, a glimpse of a stranger at a train station, for example, unlocked a world of the unconscious, where inspiration received a shape, the single point of the opening.

The point of start could mark anywhere in the story, and working backward and forward simultaneously, and standing outside, staring at it narratively, through someone's mind, someone's imagination, could be re*imaged*, until the unfolded "suggestion," the clue, existed in a narrative, a book. But a single subtlety it was wrapped up in—without words—began the process.

In a point "in the imagination" and "standing still," it held statically and at the same time in expansion—through contact with his own mind—a universe in which it eternally explained and re-enacted and re-encountered, in multiple forms, all the versions of itself that might exist, and that the author was able to "capture" in words.

So, the small, static universe of the implied story, a single mental photo, picked up alive and activated—this static universe, upon contact, instantly *expanded*. There was no stopping it, except at the end of the book—there was so much it had to say.

In miniature, this then the Big Bang, that—from its inception point—expanded. But it also stayed correctly small, exactly as at the start. The author could explain what it had been; if necessary, where the whole thing began. This then describing, in a sense, the "creative act," as what we call primarily the "right brain" grabbed the clue and let it stretch.

The mass creating the curves, in the interaction between the incipience and the unfolding in words. And this, then, even such an act as the creation of the Earth, we are told.

As reenacted in the creative act. In conjunction with the pattern for creation itself, preexisting and preestablished, in the very instant of creation's taking place, "once and forever." Until a new creative pattern was established. But the mass curled up inside the spot, the dot, the point, where it began and which it continually replayed, this creative act of making the "point," the "mark," the "dropped handkerchief" that so long ago had meant something.

In the interaction with the energy of the writer's brain, his soul, his spirit (or the woman writer's brain, soul, spirit), the creative "Act" regains initiative. It regains shape, it speaks of its origin, which creates not just the name's recording, but in fact the signature, in energy form. And that too a point, in every passage on the page, that holds the same "attraction" AS IT HAD AT THE START.

These two coupled now, joined, the point which gave the first "start" to the writer's mind and the point HE MADE. The two now one larger point, that could be shrunk back to the original point and from there re-started again. Or one could set out from where he (she) stopped. Let that be the point.

But we know the original impetus. That, preserved too. And so this imageWay into the unconscious, this "spot," this perception recorded visually, this "impression," this record left in the way that fragrance (to Proust) stimulated the mind to remember. But here a simple, *charged* image that, in encountering a mind, released energy. Something that, in being implied, held mass. The mass of the implication. "Stored" that way, clueing in the conscious mind that there was something unconsciously significant here, something, just as in any Big Bang, including that of the universe itself, in inception, leaves "something to the imagination." So in "leaving a mark," a "signature," if an Energetic Signature, what he left in fact was *something to the imagination.*

Willing it to future imaginations, that they might continue the lineage of this kind of art. Endowing the world with the significance found, by accident, in the glance cast at the pictures of life, that silently held *unrecorded information*. And in this way, not the way of the sometimes-sterile factual but of the mass-transformed, mass-mined source, returning to the Earth the fruits of its own collected works. For the energy stored in the mass mind was often recorded in a fragile glimpse of a wisp of hair that somehow revealed it held a "point." The point of its tiny universe, which meant all to itself, to someone. And this creative "explosion" that was the result created and signified the signature, that in all ways honored the inspiration it had received. That is, by exploring into the unconscious, lifting from it what it said to him was ready now, to be taken from storage.

But what are we talking about here,

BUT—TRANSFORMATION.

Like any occasion for $e = mc^2$.

AT MY EXPENSE

The old position
Old key phrase

Suppose something anticipated the curtailment of the philosophy

The step out of the old position
Watch as it happened

Why always at
(not begrudged
—*that a* human expectation)

Moving into
NOT at my expense,
how would the world look then
Not able to count on the Light (still out there in the field of
"optical astronomy"—detectable sources found in space) that
had "footed" the bill before
But that as it stepped back
hearing instead
NOT
at my expense
So that the bill arrived UNPAID
At the door of
the twenty-first century.

The archetype being left, like a shed skin
the archetype of
Let me "foot" the bill
at
my expense
Don't worry, don't look this way, don't look behind,
All that shifting into
right at the doorway, and the archetype stepped in,

Like an open bankbook for the Earth
no expense too great
no check not covered
Was it God? Christ? the Sufis, the Yogis????? all of them??
surreptitiously, subtly, latent, inert,
so that no one even noticed or thought of it; that someone
might be holding the bankbook of the earth
the very air that was breathed,
the thoughts in the air, partly purified

Mankind did not live by bread alone, but what about
bank
ROLLS
Now someone began to
think of it earnestly
was that excluded
what about
bank
ROLLS???

So, this question began to weave in from another dimension,
colliding almost—the idea that "not bread alone" was good enough
of a version, but what about if someone just substituted or added or
changed the idea to that of
bank
rolls????

But who would do it?
maybe it was the devil himself/
herself
somehow the idea said it might
get mixed up with it, that would confuse
the very idea, up there where ideas think; if someone added
into the wording of the energetics the idea that it might be
just a matter of thinking of the whole thing as
a matter of
bank
rolls

So

colli

of a

char

banl

ROI

But

Oh no, we don't think it was
anyone at all
but JUST THE POSSIBILITY THAT SOMEONE MIGHT
so many things were getting headed off
now that
they stood in the possibility chambers of
the things that would be dominating
the inhabitants of the Earth in
This one-quarter-old, almost, century

So somebody took out the bankbook of the Earth and said
no, not you
and that was how the whole thing began to shift
because if some were excluded then
the idea itself was exclusive
and as it did not want to be
it called the whole thing off
no bills paid at this time
it had to think about it
what to do, to refuse some ideas and energies entry, if
it was it
it itself that usually
hid behind the other words to really
hold out the
bank
ROLL of
THE EARTH

who held this bankbook for the Earth
We don't know but we know that something was

CHANGING

In fact, indeed, René Descartes had his dream (which inspired his life work) after sitting in a wall stove. Even, some say, thinking of the type of wall stove in those days, he'd crawled in.

It meant nothing, to me. And so could have remained. Forever, in fact. Until this thing hit me, this massive idea. And suddenly, the image, the curve, was a straight line. Absolutely straight. Just as straight as Einstein's thought patterns, when he scribbled an idea onto a piece of paper; the corner of a sheet of paper, a notecard. Just as clear as that, it was. This image was precisely not in any way a curve, but in the greatest and most elaborate of fine detail, A STRAIGHT LINE.

I take the book *Descartes' Dream: The World According to Mathematics* (New York: l Harcourt, Brace Javanovich, 1986, p. 3). It says (in the very first paragraph): "The modern world, our world of triumphant rationality, began on November 10, 1619, with a revelation and a nightmare. On that day in the small Bavarian village of Ulm, René Descartes, a Frenchman, crawled into a wall stove and, when he was well warmed, had a vision." We stop here. We read it several times before we get the meaning. So we leave it like this to wait till the appropriate page, when not just the words but the meaning itself "clicks." That is, when understanding connects to something and the curve shifts. Now we look again. We see: a straight line.

A couple more observations. And then we go.

And so we say to ourselves, very well, if in the field of patterns, then—geometrically speaking—one could, with massive-enough energy, *Change the Pattern*.

BAUDELAIRE: "Somewhere there must be a place where bread
(*le pain*) is
cake (*gâteau*)"

the tension of opposites
We will try that as location,
or place of encyclopedic information, where
they
attract

Descartes' cryptic dream "answer"
handed over now
"oui et non"

The left-brain (either/or)
the right-brain
yes and no.

So that's it
what got into Descartes' mind
in the ovenlike cavity
the stove
that's exactly it
a *tour de* FOUR*

---

* *four* = oven (Fr)

Yes,
Exactly
a tour de
FORCE

images steeling up their courage, ready to try to make it this
time, their Case
juridical
(at-the-BAR).
Suppose, suppose that the Gate AU
the "cake"
the *gâteau*
has attached
A GATE TO IT
a Gate related to
K-
OSE*

inner Universe dye-
namics
colorful enough

related to
$E = \frac{1}{2}$
mv^2
parabolically and symbolically, of course

---

* *oser* = to dare (Fr)

images lining up
READY TO SPEAK

As Descartes,

who did not sit—or wait a minute now?
depending on what was then on this plot of ground;
after all, he lived in Paris—
at this café
yet

"dweller at the outskirts of town"
has that in his name,
Des-
cartes
not to mention
men-
u
and
the |brain|map there too
the
CARTE

But this is surely getting the cart before the horse here
and before the wheel and everything else!!
yes, most definitely
a runaway
well in advance of
everything else
in our bar juridical

OUT OF THE STONE OF SCIENCE

*F*ritjof Capra (1996, *The Web of Life: A New Scientific Understanding of Living Systems*, on Ilya Prigogine, co-author of *Order Out of Chaos*):

> The conceptual shift implied in [Nobel Prize winner Ilya] Prigogine's theory [of "order through fluctuations"] involves several closely related ideas. The description of *dissipative structures* that exist *far from equilibrium* requires a *nonlinear* mathematical formalism, capable of modeling multiple interlinked feedback loops . . . When a dissipative structure reaches such a point of instability, called a *bifurcation point*, an element of *indeterminacy* enters into the theory. At the bifurcation point the system's behavior is inherently *unpredictable*. In particular, new structures of higher *order* and complexity may emerge spontaneously. Thus, self-organization, the spontaneous emergence of order, results from the combined effects of non-equilibrium, irreversibility, feedback loops, and instability.
>
> The radical nature of Prigogine's vision is apparent from the fact that these fundamental ideas were rarely addressed in traditional science and were often given negative connotations. (p. 192, italics in original text).
>
> "Today," Prigogine reflects, "[t]his convergence of two worlds [the world we see outside and

the world we see within] is perhaps one of the important cultural events of our age" (p. 193).

pp. 190–191:

The points of instability at which dramatic and unpredictable events take place, where order emerges spontaneously and complexity unfolds, are perhaps the most intriguing and fascinating aspect of the theory of dissipative structures. Before Prigogine, the only type of instability studied in some detail was that of turbulence, caused by the internal friction of a flowing liquid or gas. Leonardo da Vinci made many careful studies of turbulent flows of water, and in the nineteenth century a series of experiments was undertaken that showed that any flow of water or air will become turbulent at sufficiently high velocity—in other words, at sufficiently large "distance" from equilibrium (the motionless state).

pp. 191–192:

At the bifurcation point, . . . [a] tiny random fluctuation, *often called" "noise,"* can induce the choice of path [italics added] . . .

Thus ALL DETERMINISTIC DESCRIPTION BREAKS DOWN WHEN a dissipative structure crosses the bifurcation point. Minute fluctuations in the environment will lead to the choice of the branch it will follow. And since, in a sense, it is those random fluctuations that lead to the emergence of new forms of order, Prigogine has coined the phrase "order through fluctuations" to describe the situation [caps added].

a PK illustration:
is it noise? an electronic signal?

Harnessing, Mechanizing, DESCRIBING Chaos

⊥⊥ ◄ αί

Tolstoy—at the end of *War and Peace*: "The same contradiction seems insoluble. When committing an act I am convinced that I do it of my own freewill, but considering that action in its connexion with the general life of mankind (in its historical significance), I am convinced that this action was predestined and inevitable. Where is the error?" He went on:

> I have undoubtedly by my own will just lifted and lowered my arm. I can at once stop writing. You can at once stop reading . . . But near me stands a child and I raise my hand above him and want to lower it with the same force onto the child. I *cannot* do this. A dog rushes at that child and I *cannot refrain* from lifting my hand at the dog. I am on parade, and cannot help following the movement of the regiment . . . I *cannot* . . .

> So there are two kinds of actions: some that do and others that do not depend on my will. And the mistake causing the contradiction is due only to the fact that I wrongly transfer the consciousness of freedom (which properly accompanies every act relating to my *ego*, to the highest abstractions of existence) to actions performed in conjunction with others and dependent on the coincidence of other wills with my own. To define the limits of freedom and dependence is very difficult and the definition of those limits forms the sole and essential problem of psychology, but observing the conditions of the manifestation of our

greatest freedom and greatest dependence, we cannot but see that the more abstract and therefore the less connected with the activity of others our activity is, the more free it is; and on the contrary, the more our activity is connected with other people the less free it is (pp. 547–548, *War and Peace*).

p. 546:

A man who kills another, Napoleon who orders the crossing of the Nilemen, you or I handing in a petition to be admitted to the army, or lifting or lowering our arm, are all indubitably convinced that our every action is based on reasonable grounds and on our own freewill, and that it depends on us whether we do this or that. This conviction is so inherent in us and so precious to each of us, that in spite of the proofs of history and the statistics of crime (which convince us of absence of freedom in the actions of other people) we extend the consciousness of our freedom to all our actions.

From "Some Words about *War and Peace*" (published in *Russian Archive*, 1868): "It is a noteworthy that almost all those who have written of the campaign of 1812 have seen something special and fateful in that event. L. T." (p. 548 footnote)

The concluding paragraph: "The activity of these people [those who thought they controlled the events] interested me only as an illustration of the law of predetermination which in my opinion guides story, and of that psychological law which compels a man who commits actions under the greatest compulsion, to supply in his imagination a whole series of retrospective reflections to prove his freedom to himself" (Wordsworth Classics, 1993).

Chaos, pp. 232–233:

The boundary is where a Mandelbrot set program spends most of its time and makes all of its compromises. There, when 100 or 1,000 or 10,000 iterations fail to break away, a program still cannot be absolutely certain that a point falls inside the step. Who knows what the millionth iteration will bring? . . . The boundary is where points are slowest to escape the pull of the set. It is as if they are balanced between competing attractors, one at zero and the other, in effect, ringing the set at a distance of infinity.

When scientists moved from the Mandelbrot set itself to new problems of representing real physical phenomena, the qualities of the set's boundaries came to the fore. The boundary between two or more attractors in a dynamical system served as a threshold of a kind that seems to govern so many ordinary processes, from the breaking of materials to the making of decisions . . . . For an influential group in the early 1980s, a most promising new field of mathematics and physics was the study of fractal basin boundaries.

p. 233:

This branch of dynamics [the study of fractal basin boundaries in the early 1980s] concerned itself not with describing the final, stable behavior of a system but with the way a system chooses between competing options. A system like [Konrad] Lorenz's now-classic model ([the Butterfly Effect] has just one attractor in it, one behavior that prevails when the system settles down, and it is a chaotic attractor . . . The study of fractal basin boundaries was the study of systems that could reach one of several nonchaotic final states, raising the question of how to predict *which*. James Yorke, who pioneered the investigation of fractal basin boundaries a decade after giving chaos its name, proposed an imaginary pinball machine .

. .

This is deterministic pinball—no shaking the machine.

p. 235 (re a fractal basin boundaries figure: "For some starting conditions, the outcome is quite predictable—black is black and white is white. But near the boundary, prediction becomes impossible."

p. 245: "one of Einstein's more paradoxical gifts to physics, the notion of gravity waves rippling through the fabric of space-time."

p. 261 (Robert Shaw):

Just as turbulence transmits energy from large scales downward through chains of vortices to the dissipating small scales of viscosity, so information is transmitted back from the small scales to the large—at any rate, this was how [Robert] Shaw and his colleagues began describing it. And the channel transmitting the information upward is the strange attractor, magnifying the initial randomness just as the Butterfly Effect magnifies small uncertainties into large-scale weather patterns.

pp. 261–262:

"'Billions of years ago there were just blobs of protoplasm; now billions of years later here we are. So information has been created and stored in our structure. In the development of one person's mind from childhood, information is clearly not just accumulated but also generated—created from connections that were not there before' [said Norman Packard]. It was the kind of talk that could make a sober physicist's head spin."

p. 299 (Erwin Schrodinger):

"A living organism has the 'astonishing gift of concentrating a "stream of order" on itself, and thus escaping the decay into atomic chaos.' . . . The building block of life—it was not yet called DNA—was an *aperiodic crystal*."

p. 300:

"Schrodinger's view was unusual. That life was both orderly and complex was a truism; to see aperiodicity as the source of its special qualities verged on mystical. In Schrodinger's day, neither mathematics nor physics provided any genuine support for the idea. There were no tools for analyzing irregularity as a building block of life. Now those tools exist."

p. 308:

> Everything tends toward disorder. Any process that converts energy from one form to another must lose some as heat . . . *Entropy must always increase in the universe and in any hypothetical isolated system within it.* However expressed, the Second Law is a rule from which there seems no appeal. In thermodynamics that is true. But the Second Law has had a life of its own in intellectual realms far removed from science, taking the blame for disintegration of societies . . .
> But thermodynamic entropy fails miserably as a measure of the changing degree of form and formlessness in the creation of amino acids, of microorganisms, of self-reproducing

plants and animals, of complex information systems like the brain. Certainly these evolving islands of order must obey the Second Law. The important laws, the creative laws, lie elsewhere.

Life was found, eventually, at the bottom of the sea, that did not live through the sun. It made energy without depending on it, but rather turned toward the Earth center. With geysers of heat poured into the cold sea. An entirely different way of being INVOLVED. EVOLVED.

Cranking

Up the End

Plato:

From *Phaedrus* (p. 77):

SOCRATES: Now can we distinguish another kind of communication which is the legitimate brother of written speech, and see how it comes into being and how much better and more effective it is?

PHAEDRUS: What kind do you mean and how does it come about?

SOCRATES: I mean the kind that is written on the soul of the hearer together with understanding; that knows how to defend itself, and can distinguish between those it should address and those in whose presence it should be silent.

PHAEDRUS: You mean the living and animate speech of a man with knowledge, of which written speech might fairly be called a kind of shadow.

SOCRATES: Exactly. Now tell me this . . .

Romania: In the Cave

The cave chamber was at odds with the ritual phallus that Jung saw in his dream. We have not yet finished with this dream. Not because it is inexhaustible but because of where it is leading.

Here, in the Romanian cave, near Făgăraş, the symbols were turned around. Further back, into time, there were giant, elongated crystals placed in large holes in the cave wall. We will already introduce the concept that sound waves travel through them.

The womb of the thought patterns here
was barely drilled in
 or—like an oil well,
instead of ORWELL—
chosen for the next frontier.

We set this up in some preliminaries about structuring an **information technique** for the twenty-first century, dipping down into the Unconscious Well of humanity.*

As if the spokes were turning on the road of the old wheel—archaic as it might seem—rediscovering it on another level of itself.

Wheel/*roue* (chakra)—the nonphysical essence of the term
 alternative to ORWELL
Oui et non
Yes and no
Either/or
ORwell

The unconscious destiny, or morphology, of humankind. Rather, pardon, Earth life.

Morphology of the Earth plan. As it is still planning. Using or expressing that through human minds.

---

* *l'huile* = oil – French (pron. "we'll"; add an "h," and it's "wheel")

bC

s2Q

As I wake myself up, I will urgently write things like this, labeling it:

Freeing the Mind.

I think this has clearly gotten to, finally, in illustration, at long last, the subject of Final Cause, which, Aristotle said, everything has, gravitates toward like a flower lifting toward the sun. No, said later humanity. We do not each have a "final cause." You decide.

My life plan (well, after all, wasn't Newton investigating it, looking for it?) is, like yours, geared toward some clear, believable explication and pointers toward the understanding, the credibility of how to see FINAL CAUSE.

Something modern. worthy of having been mentioned as the very essence, of the name itself—one way to cite it, that would be completely clear—Alpha-Omega. That is, the End. Did it have a cause as a conception in itself, that had been completed, defined, expressed, created itself—in terms of a unit that could be called itself so that it was more than merely just any expression, to use the particular phrase "I am the Alpha and the Omega," but rather, some principle co-existing with and in life itself perhaps, that Newton, missing, felt terribly absent in his theory. For he had gotten the theory, but not the explanation of final cause.

Looking in the history of the Bible, he did not look in, because it was hidden somewhere *else in time*, and not in his lifetime—but wasn't it in his lifeline? this question that obsessed him? Where it was? Where was the principle of the end (as cause), that had already been specified as cryptically existing in principle—if one used the formula Alpha-Omega?

"In this movement, the 'picture' present at any given moment would consist only of aspects that can be explicated together (i. e., that correspond to a certain value of the implication parameter T" (Bohm, p. 153)

If universal, it perceives itself virtual but real in energy terms, potentially matter, even if silent or blanketed by other considerations at the moment, or otherwise, it—at least, if lacking a majority vote in all energy it encounters or where it perceives to have some voice, in setting up this planet—is in a world where it does not exist.

The same principle applies to each one. You are here to create the world in which your universality is.

Then, when one submits to other people, in their worlds, ONE DOES NOT LOSE ONESELF. It is not *either* their existence, in its primality, *or yours, in its*—but some recognition on a higher level. Where you are a world, and your totality knows that, and even here—in a physical form—however threatening to this concept in the past—YOU CANNOT BE THREATENED, so long as you focus on being yourself. Now, this news comes to me. I hasten to proclaim it. I feel the path is old, the news perhaps new. Though old too.

Bohm, p. 154: On T (collective Big Time) and *t* (small and individual): how it can be asynordinate, etc.: "These two parameters are only related in a *contingent* manner (in this case by the rate of turning of the stirring device). It is the T parameter that is directly relevant to the description of the implicate structure, and not the *t* parameter." From here, to move into all kinds of terms, constituting questions, such as of synchronous, synordinate and asynordinate ("that is, constituted of aspects with different degrees of implication").

But what were these walled-in, laid-down crystals, in shape, but the geometry of the enthroned form with the eye in the Jung dream, that opened his child mind to his work in the universal mind????? the same geometry.

HERE, there was a conjunction of evolved symbols, BY GOING FURTHER BACK. Into remembering, yes or no?

There were those who came to the Earth TO TEAR DOWN
THE ENTHRONED THREE-DIMENSIONAL
THOUGHT.

The spindled POINT OF IT ALL has just brought this
information: Here, at this radius, when it could have come AT
ONCE—AND LEFT THIS OUT—the radius has now revealed
further connections.

From the tower image, one sees Jung's second home, his
retreat at Bollingen.

> Gradually, through my scientific work, I
> was able to put my fantasies and the contents
> of the unconscious on a solid footing. Words
> and paper, however, did not seem real enough
> to me; something more was needed. I had to
> achieve a kind of representation in stone of
> my innermost thoughts and of the knowledge
> I had acquired. Or, to put it another way, I had
> to make a confession of faith in stone. That
> was the beginning of the "Tower," the house
> which I built for myself at Bollingen . . .
>
> After some time had passed—I once more
> had a feeling of incompleteness.

Yet more building occurred later:

> From the beginning . . . the Tower as in some
> way a place of maturation . . . gave me a feeling
> as if I were being reborn in stone. It is thus a
> concretisation of the individuation process, a
> memorial *aere perennius* . . . Only afterwards did
> I see how all the parts fit together and that a
> meaningful form had resulted in a symbol of
> psychic wholeness. (pp. 251–52).

One sees Jung building it; in that way, rebuilding his connection with his physical self, the one who liked to work with his hands, and concealed in that activity news of his existence and information about it. Acquaintanceship.

I see the tower he tore down as a child and rebuilt.

The radar sweeping further and capturing more that it can pick up in this intensity.

I see the first dream of Jung of the enthroned ritual phallus, shaped like an elliptical treetrunk-thick form, that was, at the top, used to see through. The eye turned to the ceiling, frozen in focus.

I see the throne-turned-tower being built and torn down, carrying the Third Eye perspective—of the Destroyer—in it.

—that thread allied to the thread of two destroying impulses: to destroy as a pathway of reconstruction..

Bearing down upon the Earth energy, this Third Eye barreled toward us. Not a meteor, but the

Third "I."

The Sleepwalkers, pp. 477–78:

In the quirks of history, Koestler identifies this as the moment that set the stage for the Inquisition attack against Galileo. He alienated the Jesuits:

> Father Grienberger, who succeeded Clavius as head of the Roman College, was to remark later that "if Galileo had not incurred the displeasure of the Company, he could have gone on writing freely about the motion of the earth to the end of his days."
>
> The clash with the Aristotelians was inevitable. The point to be established is that the attitude of the *Collegium Romanum* and of the Jesuits in general changed from friendliness to hostility, not because of the Copernican views held by Galileo, but because of his personal attacks on leading authorities of the Order.
>
> Other great scientists, including Newton, became embroiled in bitter polemics. But these were peripheral to their work, skirmishes around a solidly established position. The particular tragedy of Galileo was that his two major works were only published after his seventieth year. Up to then, his output consisted in pamphlets, tracts, manuscripts circulated privately, and oral persuasion—all of it (except the *Star Messenger*) polemical, ironically aggressive, spiced with arguments *ad hominem*. The best part of his life was spent in these skirmishes. Until the end he had no fortress in the form of a massive and solid *magnum opus* to fall back upon. The new conception of science and philosophy which he brought into the world is diffused in passages here and there among the polemics of the *Letters*

on Sunspots or *The Assayer*—hidden between
tangles of barbed wire, as Kepler's laws were
among his harmonic labyrinths. (p. 478).

Dialogues Concerning Two New Sciences, the "science of
dynamics," upon which his real fame rests, he finished in 1636,
age seventy-two. Visited by Milton in 1638 (Galileo blind in
both eyes, under house arrest). Died seventy-eight, in 1642,
the year, almost to the day, Newton was born.

Newton born Christmas Day 1642. We will stop here and
roundly, soundly, emphasize this, to come back to. Not in the
context of Christmas, per se. But something this reveals to us,
interesting in our researches. Quite definitely SO.

"The recital of the penitential psalms was delegated, with
ecclesiastical consent, to his daughter, Sister Marie Celeste,
a Carmelite nun" (p. 500); i.e., one of the punishments of
Galileo's trial.

"Kepler was the first to explain 'weight' as the *mutual
attraction* between two bodies" (p. 507); "he correctly attributed
the tides to the attraction of the sun and moon; yet, as we
saw, at the decisive moment he shrank back from the fantastic
notion of a gravitational *anima mundi*" (p. 507).

pp. 510–512 (Newton between twenty-four and forty-four):
"It is, alas, impossible to reconstruct his struggle on the rungs
of Jacob's ladder with the angel who guards the secrets of
the cosmos—as we have been able to do in Kepler's case;
for Newton was not communicative about the genesis of his
discoveries, and the scant information he provides sounds
like rationalizations after the fact."

Koestler described how he

at the same time knowingly walked into what
looked like the deadliest trap of all: action-at-
a-distance, ubiquitous, pervading the entire
universe like the presence of the Holy Ghost. The

enormity of this step can be vividly illustrated by the fact that a steel cable of a thickness equalling the diameter of the earth would not be strong enough to hold the earth in its orbit. Yet *the gravitational force which holds the earth in its orbit is transmitted from the sun across ninety-three million miles of space without any material medium to carry that force. The paradox is further illustrated by Newton's own words, which I have quoted before but which bear repeating* [italics added]:

"*It is inconceivable* [Newton wrote], *that inanimate brute matter should, without the mediation of something else, which is not material, operate upon, and affect other matter without mutual contact. And this is one reason, why I desired you would not ascribe innate gravity to me.* That gravity should be innate, inherent, and essential to matter, so that one body may act upon another, at a distance through a vacuum, **without the mediation of anything else, by and through which their action and force may be conveyed** from one to another, is to me so great an absurdity, that I believe no man who has in philosophical matters a competent faculty of thinking, can ever fall into it. Gravity must be caused by an agent acting constantly according to certain laws; but whether this agent be material or immaterial, I have left to the consideration of my readers" [emphasis added].

The "agent" to which he refers is the interstellar ether, which was supposed somehow to transmit the force of gravity. But how this is done remained unexplained; and whether the ether was something material or not, remained an open question—not only in the reader's but also in Newton's mind. He sometimes called it a medium, but on other occasions used the term "spirit." Thus the ambiguity which we noted in Kepler's use of the term "force" as a half animistic, half mechanistic concept, is equally present (though less explicitly stated) in Newton's concept of gravity.

Newton filled the entire space of the universe with interlocking forces of attraction, issuing from all particles of matter and acting on all particles of matter, across any boundless abysses of darkness. (p. 512).

Putting these pieces into this form, we see the Earth encountering A HIGHER ASPECT OF ITS OWN (we repeat, its own), its PLANETARY Third Eye form.

We see the Earth understanding that not only does the solar system NOT revolve around the Earth, THE SUN ALSO IS NOT THE CENTER OF THE UNIVERSE. The sun too is revolving AROUND A CENTER.

And that center is

THE CENTER OF A GALAXY.

WHAT DOES THIS MEAN?

It extends—by tearing down the tower—the entire three-dimensional form.

BUT AT THE SAME TIME, it sees the other side: the REBIRTH pattern.

Sees the new life, sees the child mind superseding the adult conclusion of the experience of Earth information. IT sees INTERCEPTION of the course of the Earth.

IT SEES THE EARTH COURSE SHIFTED, CHANGED.

It sees all this NOW in the compass of WHERE WE ARE, through the viewpoint of a large, large space telescope, A UNIVERSE TELESCOPE.

It redefines the meaning of LIFE ON EARTH.

NOT FINISHED

*I*t would turn out that there was a consciousness that had never become dependent on physical reality, and that was the one I was going toward. It would not be to deny or denigrate the physical, but to show it in another light. So, I was going toward the consciousness that had never completely landed here, and whose world looked nothing like this one.

It was a shock.

the two into balance. This being

Remembering that working in texts is, in another sense, at this level, sorting out the ideas and refabricating them, readying them for use, as plants make oxygen ready for us. Shifting the shape of the ideas is, on some level, preparing them for consumption. Introducing them inside formats, as when the tiny "eye" or hole at the top of the tower of the Făgăras cave made visible (after the tower fell) mere portions of objects in trickles of light—outlines, hypnotic, of what the light fell on, falling to the ground through the one hole: objects the darkness inside the cave had hidden when the view had been lit by matches.

Indicating to the people inside that they were contacting the vastness of the starry heavens above, that let these rays, not cosmic but sending outlines into the earth in any case, into their inner rituals.

> That there are two versions [the Heisenberg/ Schrodinger dispute] of atomic physics should come as no surprise, because in our world of perceptions things come in pairs, such as particles and waves, yin and yang, black and white, yes and no, love and hate, light and darkness—there are no intrinsic maybes as there are in the atomic world . . . [I]n our personal lives . . . we generally try to resolve ambiguous situations through decisiveness— once again, into an "either/or" mode. As Einstein and Picasso demonstrated in the first decade of the twentieth century, ambiguity is the key to discovering representations (p. 100, Arthur I. Miller, in Farmelo, ed.).

And after all my speculation, let us return now to this confounding new statement I have already introduced, to take it further:

> Not only can two events be correlated, linking the earlier one to the later one, but *two events can become correlated such that it becomes impossible to say which is earlier and which is later.*

This seems completely preposterous. It requires, of course, that we disconnect ourselves from linear time. When I imagined far-distant events connected in Event Balls, I had no idea at all to suggest that what caused the connection might not be a straightforward plan from the Other Side. It was too mysterious to grant any other explanation. To go on:

Each of these events is the cause of the other,

Imagine.

as if each were the first to occur.[15]

280

So, let's take a look at the lifeline—the timeline, as I experienced it—of the dream I had of a car accident in 1981. I deduced later it introduced a relay race of "Go" signals: appearing then but as a *symbol* of the death by cancer of Milton Klonsky later that year. But the dream did not fit Milton's details except as an announcement of impending death. But they did fit the death ten years later of my boyfriend/housemate in an *actual* car accident, as if the dream got into the wrong time slot, or as if—is that possible?—I was seeing the future car-accident death *because* it was somehow precipitated, announced (ordered? assured?) by the first death? This is a ridiculous situation—if we have lineups of deaths (or of any sequence of events). We have never hypothesized such a thing: events lining up in a relay, ready to take the Olympic flame down to the Earth. I have never heard of it. But the idea grew on me, or smashed into me.

In 1991 the literal car-wreck death—it too was preceded by a car-accident dream, this one terribly frightening. A friend, Russell Park (literally Russell Park, PhD), dreamed it in our apartment, finding it so chillingly real he toyed with the idea of rejecting Willy's offer to drive him to the Brussels airport—better act odd and call a taxi—scared the crash would manifest en route. In this period, other uncanny warnings were occurring, so that Willy had the conviction he was trying to "outrun death"; then *even as* he was dying *unknown to me*, I dreamed of packing up, moving from Belgium to the United States *to work on "The Hunter Thompson Story."*

The first dream, in 1981, was a symbol, a metaphor. Or it was a precognitive image attached to the 1981 death? But why? By what hook? What created the appendage? We see no "cause." But information cloaked in many dreams told me Milton was ill.

So how did a car accident fit? Why depicted in that guise? As a metaphor? Then came a real death by car accident ten years later, as if the first instance had been amplified into a literal accident, the second in the chain.

For a multitude of reasons, I deduced the two occurrences

must be connected. *Outlandish*, I told myself. There was no logic to it. Not even a single strain. First, introduce the symbol, then put it, like worked-on clay, down into matter ten years later. Yet I held on to the idea this was an Event Ball.

What gauntlet had been thrown down? Or series of men "running the gauntlet"?

In the 1981 dream, a willowy, El Greco-like figure, stretched into a soul-, other worldly form like in the Toledo museum, seemingly anticipated, unflinching, the decision to die in the accident ten years later. In some sort of sacrifice, I deduced. It drove home to me the question whether this was a relay of purposeful deaths, his intention unconscious, ending in the moment when (at the bottom of Greek Temple steps in the dream) he disappeared completely. Greco, Greek temple. I never figured out that connection.

But with no one the wiser consciously in 1991, all Willy's friends had their bristles up; this single-car accident was suspicious. They all said so. A psychic I trusted later told me a fact that explained the willowy appearance of the figure in the crash in the 1981 dream. She said Willy was out of body when the accident occurred. Suspicious indeed. A sacrifice, yes.

Now the connections were getting more bizarre but also as if shouting. Only a lunatic would see connections in these disparate events. Yet they forced into my head the term "event balls." *As if time unfolded events from a balled-up fist into our time-sequenced world.* In ways so obscure, so winding we could never follow them to all the outlets called events in our world; as if events, outside their Earth timing, had interconnected highways and implications. Like flung-down fireballs. The connections announcing themselves in advance in dreams and other subtle-energy means.

Linked events connect, I speculated, so that when one occurs, no matter where, no matter when, the other is mysteriously, determinedly "set to Go"—not even tangentially to our eyes related to it. I have no idea, to this day, exactly how this works, except in subtle energy the connections led one to the other, underscored by fatal outcomes.

But somewhere, somehow strung together, when there is no "cause" that we know of creating a relationship. E*xcept—yes. This one, of entanglement that (apparently, guesswork and theory tell us) took place invisibly.* Certainly in ways we are not privy to, yet living inside us humans. Destroying with a sledgehammer the concept of linear time. No, these chains worked precognitively.

Again, as Arthur I. Miller wrote, "Not only can two events be correlated, linking the earlier one to the later one, but *two events can become correlated such that it becomes impossible to say which is earlier and which is later.*"

Earlier, finding the glimmerings of this idea, all alone, intuitively, not as physics theory, I hadn't been able to shake it.

Yes, these events seem to fall, each linked to the other *in an intention.* Launching "Go" signals like spaceships sent out to far planets, arriving at now you, now me, through unseen hook-ups we have *with an event experienced by someone else*! Intentions, purposes, so deep they might override no matter what else is going on in our lives, might line up not immediately—but ten years later.

Yet this would have to mean events were purposeful. Some were. Events themselves, like us, incarnated by us.

The only link I can find is consciousness, purpose—service if you will—an intent made before birth. Heavens. Yes, heaven is in on it.

Well, what will they tell us next, these quantum speculations? What exciting principles, once we make "space-time"—which doesn't exist except as derived from the matter in it—for them?

But did I not write in this book: "For here we are, on the borderline of an understanding in which things *superimpose*. The awareness that, then, even now has a certain degree of space in my brain—this moment on top of that one"? That too, we can stack up in our compilation of new principles, new ideas to ruminate over, to put into the pot being stirred and sometime poured over us

All *that counts on us for*
solution-processing—
experiential inner reality manufacturing—
imprimaturs of our uniqueness
—our personal crossword puzzles of Self—

we are

meant to

fabricate

Down Here.

ACKNOWLEDGMENTS

*T*o the wise old souls I have known and learned from. To all the friends who have walked with me on this journey of Life. Thank you for being there, and may we have more adventures and discoveries. In terms of this book, I particularly thank my LuminEssence co-journeyers, and the energy provided for this book by its co-founder Duane Packer and his guide DaBen. Also to the spirit groups that work with his teachings and sustained me, opening doors while I wrote. Also, to the co-founder, Sanaya Roman and Orin. Also, to the leading-edge scientists, whose original minds I quoted. And to my friends in Belgium, in the NCDI dance studio here in Raleigh, and in parts of the United States and abroad, including Jyoti and Russel Park in California. And Ani Moriarty in France, who provided healing while I underwent my surprise "makeover" (dimensional shift) in 2022. And to my family here in North Carolina. To Ron Whitehead, who was the first to read this revised manuscript and plugged into the energies, immediately, resonating them back in a comforting and stimulating electricity. To Jef Crab, who provided his searing mind and spirit as an initial reader, reactor; when he began sending me short audio comments slowly, as he read, I realized it was a treasure to be included in the book. And to Deborah at Illumination Graphics for the design, as to Grant Goodwine for his fabulous artistic vision of the cover. Thanks to all of you. May we all impact life and each other. Continue to.

AFTERWORD

Reading Tools
and Helpful Insights for Integrating
the Text

Jef Crab,

Taoist, Tai Chi master, Rainforest activist

To hear these messages from Jef in audio by him, go to

Chapter Three

Note 003

Now, to conclude Chapter Three. The suggestions you are putting forth, especially in these last few pages—in my opinion and my feeling, they are very correct and they will help people understand those issues much better. Once again, I would like to emphasize that just as you started with Newton's ideas of gravity, and so on—mechanistic physics and Cartesian thinking—*we've evolved to a deeper understanding that actually it's not the brain that is translating all this information coming to us.* Through experiencing many years of Tai Chi now and as I developed E.A.S.T. and the principles interwoven into that method, I started understanding more and more that energy, information, and movement are always one. They are a unity. Information is not separated from energy is not separated from movement. And actually, the translation of new information always happens through the heart center, through the head center, which we call brain, and through the hara, or Dantien, where it becomes a movement. Only then it becomes meaningful to us.

I connect this idea to what I said before about holistic thinking; that actually the word "thinking" there is not correct because it is not happening only in the brain. It is a process in our larger Dan Tien—or our energetic sphere, you could call it—and the energy surrounding us, which is composed of the radiation of the heart, the head, and the belly: the three centers. Whenever they are very well aligned, they will form energetic fields, which we are well able to use in the martial arts. So, what you described about Bohm, that he was able to perceive new information through very small muscle changes, to me, is very correct, and this is what I am teaching. I teach people to become aware of these deep muscular changes, which is an indication of new energy, new information, new movement, entering our—for the time being, I would call it our personal sphere.

Chapter Four
Note 004
Regarding holistic memory:

This is happening more and more because we are slowly moving toward that level. We can absorb information better and understand information even just from, as I said, a small fragment of it. We will be able to do this more and more for the simple reason—it's also stated on p. 13—that actually this information is already in our cells, and whenever we touch that source, it is possible to enter this state of mind.

Chapter Nine
Note 006

There are a lot of very interesting ideas in Chapter 9.

I would like to elaborate where you explain that information should change our vibration and our entanglement. In the E.A.S.T. method I teach that information, energy, and action, or you could say result, are always connected. And, indeed, we consciously try to transform lower vibration into higher vibration. Whenever we sink down into a lower vibration, we give indicators, in our whole body. There are subtle indicators even before stress reaches the muscular level.

You described how Hunter and Klonsky weren't affected by the energy around them, because it's a fact, if we do nothing, we will "sink to the lowest common denominator." On the other hand, if a transformation is not put into movement, into an action, there will be no connection to the environment. The transformation will only happen inside the individual. So, in this way we are not only individuals; also, on our own and in the midst of a dialogue, a conversation with others, we can influence the environment, the collective. I think this is illustrated in this chapter. I'm happy to read that both Hunter and Klonsky experienced what influence the people around them had on their vibration.

Chapter Nine
Note 6 bis_

Jef mentions his two closest teachers:

Jóska Soós de Sóvar, the well-known Hungarian shaman with roots to Siberian Shamanism,

and Akira Tasumura, Zen master and world-famous painter and Ikebana teacher.

Regarding the idea you were expressing about creation working through people's consciousness, you are well aware that from a shamanistic point of view every human being is part of the Earth. I often explain this to my students/apprentices by comparing it to a Mandelbrot symmetry. Thus, we are not only part of the Earth, but *on an unimaginable scale we are entangled* with the Earth.

Everything that happens in human beings will happen in the Earth, and everything that happens in the Earth itself will happen in human beings, and all the other species, of course, because we are one ecosystem.

Continuing on with what I explained in note 6 about changing the vibration. This is the reason why we can be aware of sensations—*literally indicators*, allowing us the sensation of feeling a pleasant or an unpleasant event or situation. Those indicators also allow us to distinguish the difference between the two.

Already during my apprenticeship I used to ask myself: "Why did nature make a distinction only between these two: a pleasant and an unpleasant feeling or situation?"

After years of research, and the training of Jóska and Akira, I think the conclusion [is] that these indicators are directly connected to the deeper level—what you call the ultraviolet sphere—of the planet and communicate directly with it. This happens constantly, but for the superficial mind undoubtedly unconsciously.

Whenever we are in an unpleasant situation, actually there is a *request* originating from the ultraviolet sphere of the planet.

It is not to make us feel bad or make our life bad, but there is a request, namely to raise the vibration. The indicators tell us: "You shouldn't go down to this low level of vibration." Whether this happens consciously or unconsciously or willingly or unwillingly, whenever we find ourselves in an unpleasant situation, it is only a request from the creative energies of the planet to raise the vibration.

As we noticed in very evolved persons, beings like the Dalai Lama, Akira, or Jóska, after a certain time they are able to remain in a certain level of high vibration—depending on the level of the person, in this way influencing actually the whole Earth and all of humanity. One difference is that a single person of a high development will have a much greater influence because it's conscious action. As I mentioned in 006, conscious action has a much larger impact on the collective consciousness than an unconscious action.

This is why even when a lot of people go through war and thus very unpleasant situations, they do not influence the collective that much. Although they find it unpleasant, they don't find the creative Force in themselves to change it. They are not influencing the collective sphere as much as one person acting consciously and connected to the deeper level of Earth's mind. The difference lies maybe 1 to 100,000—on such a scale. Maharishi Yogi said that one person, in a very conscious way, in a very strong way, could influence a whole city. I don't know if these are exact numbers I'm calling out.

But, for sure, a person acting very consciously will affect and transform the ultraviolet sphere of the Earth/deeper mind, especially if—using your point—the transformation results in a conscious action. I emphasize here the fact that something physically in the material world has to change, whether it's digging a hole in the garden or creating an organization. It is doing something physically.

CAVES, Walls, and Begged Questions
Note 007

The chapter "Caves, Walls, and Begged Questions" is also very interesting. I was talking in note 6 about putting things into action, which is actually what you are doing with your book—acting also not only on the readers but as well on the collective consciousness. By the end of the chapter, you quote an extract of Stan Gooch, on the mind.

There is something I often discuss with neurologists as well and with psychologists, psychologists, about the functioning of the brain, and indeed we do not understand the brain that far anyway. Again, if we see this from a Taoist point of view, the brain is functioning on the lowest level of our existence: Li is actually connected with matter. Chi is connected to the energy level; the I and the Jing—the latter is the capability to move from inner, elastic force—are connected to consciousness. Then what about Shen, what we commonly translate as spirit? Again, these five levels of consciousness are also connected with the five axes [see note 8].

Now, from my experience, when we look at the three centers of consciousness—the three Dantien [mind, heart, belly]—of course, we have thinking, which is located in the head and many times especially in Western science correlated with the function of the brain. In fact, it's the opposite: the brain is functioning *because* of the *head center*. The head center is our ability to match images with the subtle information-energy impulses captured or received by the heart center. You might say, it sticks photos to our impressions in such a way we understand what is needed.

For the superficial mind, functioning at the level of Li, these photos are mostly just repetitions of former experiences. The deep mind, connected with the I or Shen, will produce complete new images. Hence the evolution of ideas and humanity.

It creates images from the energy that is already accepted by the heart center. At first, the heart, then these images rise into the head center, where the new information will be transformed into images. That's also the reason why or might be a reason why Jung had these visions. As you indicate, indeed these are visions.

As you know, whenever we have a waking dream, a vision, it is a function of very strong energy coming through the heart center and really overtaking the functioning of the brain and the overtaking of superficial memory. The images and the photographs, we store somewhere in our back.

Indeed, there is this very interesting idea you bring in by Stan Gooch. And this is in my opinion also something that has driven Western psychology in the wrong direction—about the location of the *sub*consciousness. As a matter of fact, the cerebellum is directly connected to a deep layer of our being that extends far beyond the physical level of our brain. In fact, it is a *supra*consciousness, it is beyond the physical body.

In our evolutionary process we didn't have all the senses we have today. So, even in the first life forms, these organisms had to rely on the sense of their environment, their direct connection and entanglement, and whenever something changed on the level of vibration, they were able to distinguish it and in some way connect with it, and sometimes even completely merge with it, just as you describe in Chapter 9. That new information can be merged from the entanglement, or it happens that these subatomic structures indeed merge on a certain level of the bits and the bytes, the 1s and the 0s.

Or—say, it was a hostile force—then we would retract from it and disconnect from this environment. So, it's not really the word "*sub*conscious"; that's the wrong direction because a lot of people are looking *deep* inside themselves. In fact, it's outside. For most people, it's more than one arm's length away from their body. But, as you described earlier, there are people connected even on opposite sides of the universe not in their sub- but in their supraconsciousness, people who are trained enough to feel this outer level of activity, people connected over long distances, in the entanglement of subatomic structures, even on opposite sides of the universe; this not *sub*conscious but *supra*consciousness can extend extremely far into the universe. This also explains why we say that shamans travel into different galaxies, maybe connected like to civilizations like Sirius.

Of course, this is a small change in mind we need to make: instead of from the *sub-* going to the *supra-*. I don't know if this makes any sense, but I wanted to share it. I look forward to reading more and I'm enjoying very much this conversation.

Creativity:
Back to the point
the One-Pointed Focus
Jef has a plethora of comments for this section.
Note 008

This is about the three to four pages ending with "At My Expense."

These are very provocative and thought-provoking. For instance, that Einstein rejected the concept of the expanding or contracting state of the universe.

You might be aware that in shamanism we distinguish five different axes [see note 7]; this has to do with everything you write in here. And I will come back to Einstein later on.

The first axis is in the human body; the second axis is in and through the earth; the third one from the North Pole to the Polar Star. The fourth one is in the multidimensionality, and the fifth one is in and through the primordial sound, as Jóska explained it.

There, we have to imagine that beyond the primordial sound (so beyond/before the vibration), there is a void, a nothing, an emptiness which is not an emptiness. Actually, it's as a seed waiting to sprout. It's the state of the universe where the whole universe will express itself.

In Taoism, also in Buddhism, but in Taoism they call this the *wu-chi* state of the universe, *wu-chi* meaning no life force, opposed to *tai chi*, which means great life force. In shamanism, as well as Taoism and Buddhism we accept the idea that both states, the *wu-chi* and the *tai chi*, exist at the same moment, always. This is why I started with the five axes, because they always exist at the same time.

We are part of the earth. We are in a Mandelbrot symmetry with the earth. But we are also in a Mandelbrot symmetry with

the universe because the Earth belongs to the universe; the

planetary system and the solar system really belong to the universe. So, it's all very entangled. And the same principles are working on all levels.

Note 008-2

I make this jump to Faulkner but also to creativity, where you very correctly close the last sentence: This is "transformation, like any occasion for e=mc²."

These are very very deep things you are writing here, about the origin of thought and the way creativity works through us, because if all these five axes exist simultaneously, all these levels of the universe, this means that at any given time we are able to tap into the deeper one, the creative one, even before the primordial sun, because already the manifestation is happening on a deep level through the multidimensionality, which probably today we call the quantum physical world, and then later on directed through energies, the energetic world, . . . eventually manifesting into matter, into our world.

But the same goes for thoughts. This is very related.

We also in the martial arts in general, but especially in Tai Chi, distinguish between the five different states of our muscular tissue through movement. The first one is a contracting; this is the most superficial; then there is relaxing, releasing; this is already a conscious action. The third one is a stretching; this requires a lot of exercise and technique; the fourth one is unstretching, and it will only come over time. The fifth is very deep. These five states of our muscular tissue are very connected to the five axes and to the five states of the ying of the universe.

But it likewise works in this way through our thinking process; indeed, like the fallen-hunter scene or other things you are describing, some situations can provoke a lot of thinking and a lot of movement on this level. I go back to the muscular state of mind and acting. For most people, they will only be able—only ninety percent will act from this first state of contracting muscles in order to move around; it requires a lot of exercise to do this energy, frankly, like Tai chi masters, Buddhists, shamans, on a physical level as well as on the level of the mind and the spirit. And these are very connected. But (what Jóska and Akira were teaching their students) it also means that at any given point, at any given time, we can use these axes and these states of mind, these states of being of the universe—we can enter them, we can literally vibrate in harmony with them and at that moment enter the common channel for these creative forces.

Note 008-3

Another thought was going through my mind while I was reading further. In E*ternal Spring: Living in a World of Abundance*, I wrote that at the time when Einstein was thinking about the unified field theory, he had already accepted consciousness, or mind, as a force; he had already long ago discovered and proved its existence. He felt that it was a reality, that it had to be.

But I think that most of his contemporaries weren't open to that idea. People like Jung and Bohm were different, but most of his fellow scientists, they didn't take him seriously anymore, on this idea, at Princeton even.

But Einstein knew. For sure, he knew. We have to start now to explore other options, seeing that opposite states of the universe can exist simultaneously, and this is also in Quantum Mechanics—not only the Mandelbrot symmetries, which is a very interesting idea, exist, but also, the string theory, which is interesting, entanglement—that they all exist simultaneously.

It's only a possibility, and it depends on the way you look at it. But beyond that is a unified field, which expresses all these states of being, all these states of emanation. They all exist simultaneously on *this* side of the primordial sun.

On the other side is probably a dark hole. Once we travel through the dark hole, probably on the other side you would find the real universe. All the light disappears from this side but expands on the other side.

That's my idea; it's also how Tamas Bacsi—the teacher of Jóska, the shaman blacksmith of Jóska's village in Hungary—actually explained it: that the universe was full of wormholes and passages, etc.; that one could travel from one universe to the other—in the mind, of course. And Jóska told me he was able to express himself multidimensionally on sixteen levels.

Note 00-9

Out of the Stone of Science

Related to "Out of the Stone of Science,"— "Stone of Wisdom," maybe—again, I'm very interested by all the things you're connecting to each other here.

As I already wrote in my blurb, actually, this is like a roadmap to the universe but also connected to the deep psychology of the human being, as you very well describe. Also, a very important thing here, just to clarify something more, is the principle in martial arts, and I'm talking about the Japanese tradition, what they call *muga mushin*, the empty mind; this, is connected to the fifth state of being of the universe, beyond the primordial sun. Warriors in the samurai period—they put a lot of effort into reaching this point. You find it today in things like bow and arrow shooting, the Ikebana (flower arrangement), the painting on rice paper, but especially in *jujutsu*, the martial arts, because in this state of mind they were very serious with their opponents. They were, like, completely blank. This *muga mushin* [no mind] state of mind has to be understood as completely blank and as effortless as possible. This is what you describe in the book.

We have this manifested universe where new things come in, and then things have to change, but there is something beyond it. This is what Tolstoy described in *War and Peace*—what I call the line of evolution in *Eternal Spring*—that everything on this planet follows this line of evolution.

This doesn't mean we don't have a free will to connect to this line of evolution or *not* to connect, to separate ourselves from it. But one will lead to more entropy, chaos, and the other to more harmony. This depends on how much we connect to this line of evolution. As you write, there must have been something ordering the molecules and the atoms from this protoplasm in the deep ocean to these life forms we have now. It is ridiculous to understand it as mere principles.

OK. That's about it for now.

DICTIONARY OF
MULTILINGUAL TERMS

verser (Fr) = to pour; *verre* (Fr) = glass; *ver* (Fr) = worm; *vert* (Fr) = green (these last three are pronounced the same)

trou (Fr) = hole

arm (D) = poor

en bas (Fr) = below

gâteau (Fr) = cake

arrête (Fr) = stop

domingo (Sp) = Sunday

dés (Fr) = dice

oui et non (Fr) = yes and no

four (Fr) = oven (pronounced "foor")

ose (Fr) = dare; *os* (Fr) = bone

carte (Fr) = map

NOTES

1. Quoted from the website of the late F. David Peat, http://www.muc. de/~heuvel/bohm; Peat, *Infinite Potential: The Life and Times of David Bohm*: 35ff.

2. *Infinite Potential*: 68; quoted from Peat's website.

3. *Infinite Potential*: 152.

4. *Infinite Potential*: 154.

5. Ibid.

6. "The Large and the Small," from Ford, *The World of Elementary Particles*, 1963, in Ferris, edited: 31–32.

7. Ford, "The Large and the Small": 30.

8. Ford, "The Large and the Small": 18.

9. *Quanta Magazine*, "Quantum Mischief Rewrites the Laws of Cause and Effect," https://www.quantamagazine.org/quantum-mischief-rewrites-the-laws-of-cause-and-effect-20210311/.

10. Michael Brooks, https://www.newscientist.com/article/mg25634080-300-carlo-rovelli-on-the-bizarre-world-of-relational-quantum-mechanics/.

11. Natalie Wolchover, "Time's Arrow Traced to Quantum Source," in *Quanta* magazine, Time's Arrow Traced to Quantum Source (d2r55xnwy6nx47. cloudfront.net).

12. "What Was the Relationship between Einstein and Minkowski?" https:// hsm.stackexchange.com/questions/9975/what-was-the-relationship-between-einstein-and-minkowski#:~:text=Minkowski%20was%20 one%20of%20Einstein's,had%20been%20a%20real%20lazybones.

13. George Musser, "Quantum Weirdness Now a Matter of Time," in Thomas Lin, ed., *Alice and Bob Meet the Wall of Fire*.

14. https://alleninstitute.org/what-we-do/brain-science/news-press/ articles/5-unsolved-mysteries-about-brain?gclid=CjwKCAjw-

rOaBhA9EiwAUkLV4jfD6mh8bhEH-8wxCRPvzCNrBDZEvINl9ggvprW qIYm6cqkTVJmQGRoCLkAQAvD_BwE.

15. Musser, "Quantum Weirdness Now a Matter of Time."

REFERENCES

BOHM, David (1980/1983). *Wholeness and the Implicate Order*. London: Routledge/Ark Paperbooks.

———. "Second Lesson: Quanta." In Carlo Rovelli (2016). Riverhead Books Kindle edition. *Seven Lessons on Physics*.

BROOKS, Michael. "Carlo Rovelli on the Bizarre World of Relational Quantum Mechanics." *Carlo Rovelli on the bizarre world of relational quantum mechanics | New Scientist*.

CAPRA, Fritjof (1996/1997). *The Web of Life: A New Scientific Understanding of Life*. New York: Anchor Books.

CHOWN, Marcus (2001). *The Universe Next Door: Twelve Mind-Blowing Ideas from the Cutting Edge of Science*. London: Headline Book Publishing.

DAVENPORT, Marcia. (1932/1995). *Mozart*. New York: Barnes & Noble.

DAVIS, Philip J. & HEERSH, Reuben (1986). *Descartes' Dream: The World According to Mathematics*. New York: Harcourt Brace Jovanovich.

EINSTEIN, Albert. "Autobiographical notes": 577–589. In Ferris, T., ed.

———. "$E = mc^2$": 56–59. In Ferris, T., ed.

ELSASSER, Walter M. (1987/1988). *Reflections on a Theory of Organisms: Holism in Biology*. Baltimore & London: The Johns Hopkins Univ. Press.

FERRIS, Timothy, ed. (1991). *The World Treasury of Physics, Astronomy, and Mathematics*. Boston: Little, Brown & Co.

———. FERRIS, Timothy (1997/1998). *The Whole Shebang: A State-of-the Universe(s) Report*. New York: Simon & Schuster/Touchstone.

FARMELO, Graham, ed. (2002). *It Must Be Beautiful: Great Equations of Modern Science*. London: Granta Books.

FORD, Kenneth W. "The large and the small": 18–37. In Ferris, T., ed.

GALISON, Peter. "The Sextant Equation: $E = mc^2$." In Farmelo, ed.

GLEICK, James. (1987/1988). *Chaos: Making a New Science* (9th printing). New York: Viking Penguin.

———. (1992). *Genius: The Life and Science of Richard Feynman*. New York: Pantheon Books.

GREENE, Brian (1999/2000). *The Elegant Universe: Superstrings, Hidden Dimensions, and the Quest for the Ultimate Theory*. New York: Random House/Vintage Books.

GOOCH, Stan. (1980). *The Double Helix of the Mind: The Secrets of Mental Evolution and Advance*. London: Wildwood House, Ltd.

GOSWAMI, Amit (2000). *The Visionary Window: A Quantum Physicist's Guide to Enlightenment*. Wheaton, ILL: Theosophical Publishing House/Quest Books.

HARRELL, Margaret. A. (1996-1998). *Love in Transition*, Vols. I–IV. Sibiu, Romania: Hermann Press.

————. (2002). *Space Encounters*, Vols. I–II. Sibiu, Romania: Sæculum University Press.

JUNG, Carl. G. (1961/1993). *Memories, Dreams, Reflections*. Recorded & edited by Aniela Jaffé (Richard & Clara Winston, trans.). London: Fontana Press.

————. (1959). *The Basic Writings of* C. G. *Jung*. Ed. V. S. de Laszlo. New York: Modern Library.

KANE, Gordan (2001). *Supersymmetry: Unveiling the Ultimate Laws of Nature*. Cambridge: Helix Books.

KLONSKY, Milton (1974). "Art & life: A Menippean paean to the flea; or, did Dostoevsky kill Trotsky?" In Solotaroff, T., ed., *American Review* 20: 115–188. New York: Bantam Books. Reissued (text without visuals) in Solotaroff, T., ed. (1991). A *Discourse on Hip: Selective Writings of Milton Klonsky*. Detroit, MICH: Wayne State Univ. Press.

KOESTLER, Arthur (1959). *The Sleepwalkers. London*: Arcana.

KRISHNA, Gopi (with James Hillman, Psychological Commentary) (1997). *Kundalini: The Evolutionary Energy in Man*. Boston & London: Shambhala.

Oxford Family Encyclopedia. (1997). New York: Oxford University Press. London: George Philip.

LIN, Thomas, ed. (2018). *Alice and Bob Meet the Wall of Fire: Quanta Science Stories*. Kindle, Cambridge, MASS: The MIT Press.

Miller, Arthur I. (2002) "Erotica, aesthetics and Schrödinger's wave equation." In Graham FARMELO, ed. *It Must Be Beautiful: Great Equations of Modern Science*. London, UK: Granta Books.

MUSSER, George (2018). "Quantum Weirdness Now a Matter of Time. In Thomas Lin, ed., *Alice and Bob Meet the Wall of Fire: Quanta Science Stories*.

TOMPA, Rachel. "5 unsolved mysteries about the brain." Neuroscience at the Allen Institute. https://alleninstitute.org/what-we-do/brain-science/news-press/articles/5-unsolved-mysteries-about-brain?gclid=CjwKCAiAheacBhB8EiwAltVO2yg27Tlh-CHfybAxiMpXy24dnALJ-q_sdBN8PHsz0TDiWKjPMebRGRoC57gQAvD_BwE.

PEAT, F. David (1997). New York: Basic Books, *Infinite Potential: The Life and Times of David Bohm*.

PLATO (1995). *Phaedrus* (W. Hamilton, trans.). London: Penguin 60s Classics.

———. (1965/1967). *Timaeus and Critias* (Desmond Lee, trans.). London: Penguin Classics.

RINPOCHE, Sogyal (1994). *The Tibetan Book of Living and Dying*. San Francisco: HarperOne, a division of Harper Collins.

ROVELLI, Carlo (2002). http://www.livingreviews.org/Articles.

———. "The Granularity of the World: Quanta" in *Helgoland: Making Sense of the Quantum World*, by Rovelli, Riverhead Books, Kindle, 0221.

SEDGWICK, John P. Jr. (1966). *Discovering Modern Art: The Intelligent Layman's Guide to Painting from Impressionism, to Pop*. New York: Random House

SHLAIN, Leonard (1991). *Art & Physics: Parallel Visions in Space, Time & Light*. New York: William Morrow & Co./Quill.

SMOLIN, Lee (2000/2001). *Three Roads to Quantum Gravity*. New York: Basic Books.

SMOOT, George, & Davidson, Keay (1993). *Wrinkles in Time: The Imprint of Creation*. London: Little, Brown & Co.

TAYLOR, Jeremy (1998). *The Living Labyrinth: Exploring Universal Themes in Myths, Dreams, and the Symbolism of Waking Life*. Mahwah, NJ: Paulist Press.

PRAISE FOR MARGARET HARRELL'S BOOKS

Poetry

Particle Piñata Poems

"The time of the grandmothers, of the nurturing healing feminine energy has arrived. Patriarchy has sewn destruction long enough. We must all, female and male, become healers, seers. In her epic PARTICLE PIÑATA, author Margaret Ann Harrell stands in direct lineage with the desert mystics, the poet prophets of old and, simultaneously, with the contemporary cutting edge avant-garde. In a whirling dance with the creative forces of the universe Harrell draws explicit and implicit lines to Rumi, Blake, Yeats, Joyce, Jung, and others while forging mystical connections with clouds and coastlines, dancing in the borderlands of space and time, of being and not being, of embracing and letting go. And she accomplishes it all in her own distinctly original poetic voice. Through decades of carrying these poems from continent to continent, Margaret Ann Harrell has continued to add new poems and photos, to edit and revise, to transform her self into an ever evolving being, into this masterpiece book. I can't recommend it highly enough. Go ahead, open the front cover and enter. You'll never be the same."
 —Ron Whitehead, U.S. National Beat Poet Laureate 2020–'22

"The poetry of Margaret Ann Harrell reads like a Zhuangzi of the 21st century, taking its reader through a spiritual Odyssey, where one can hear the cosmic beat in the rhythm of the word play, the pulse of heartfelt mind-blowing experiences revealing a vast span of messages from beyond. It shows the craftmanship of a female shaman who has the power to catch such a dazzling wild and free roaming content into the nets of poems. Here is a biopic in words, a biographical epic, a story of a lifetime full of surprising leaps into the story of Earth and the Cosmic Drama, a rite de passage (read the passage) initiating its reader into multiversal dimensions, bringing meaning to life where few have been looking to find it. This great bold poetry full of wit and spirit reads as a unique treat, a gift from those who know how to sow the seed for what really matters on earth: a choice to live a life guided by love and light. For those who are in love with poetry, share this genuine gift and the sheer joy of it! If you want to, go ahead!"

—Chris Van de Velde (MA Philosophy, lover of wisdom), Belgium

Other Books

The Hell's Angels *Letters: Hunter S. Thompson, Margaret Harrell and the Making of an American Classic*
(available only at Norfolk Press: norfolkpress.com)

"Thompson's motto might well have been 'Nothing in moderation.' For *The* Hell's Angels *Letters*, Margaret Ann Harrell—in collaboration with Ron Whitehead—has assembled a dossier of all her correspondence with Thompson during the time she worked as the editor of the gonzo writer's 'strange and terrible saga of the outlaw motorcycle gangs.' Typed manuscript pages, scribbled notes, photographs, interviews and all sorts of period ephemera relating to Hell's Angels allow the reader a valuable, behind-the-scenes glimpse into the making of this classic of New Journalism."

—Michael Dirda, the *Washington Post*

"As the title implies, this book is mainly comprised of letters between Harrell and Thompson, some typed and some handwritten, and all printed here in color. Of course, there are already two collections of Hunter Thompson's letters available, but somehow they are even more enjoyable when read in the original form. Whether typed or scrawled in giant letters with a red pen, Thompson's correspondence is invariably annotated and corrected in his unique way, adding a layer of personality that was missing from the collections, as well—of course—as Harrell's explanations that provide further insight."

—David Wills, *Beatdom*

"A *big book, literally and figuratively* . . . *The Hell's Angels Letters* is a must-have text for any Hunter S. Thompson fan. Lavishly documented and illustrated with the actual correspondence that led to the publication of his breakthrough literary effort . . . The author, Margaret Harrell, who was Thompson's editor on his inaugural book, and her collaborator, Thompson's friend and associate poet Ron Whitehead, have succeeded brilliantly to create a fabulous present for you, or anyone in your life who admires Thompson's numerous achievements . . . It's worth every penny. *The* Hell's Angels *Letters: Hunter S Thompson, Margaret Harrell and the Making of an American Classic* gets five stars out of five! Bravo!"

—Kyle K. Mann, *Gonzo Today*

The *Keep This Quiet!* Series

Keep This Quiet! I: My Relationship with Hunter S. Thompson, Milton Klonsky, and Jan Mensaert

"Addictive" and "a delight."

—Mark Strand, U.S. Poet Laureate 1990–'91

"Margaret Harrell's *Keep This Quiet!* offers an illuminating look at Hunter S. Thompson in full throttle trying to make it as a Top Notch prose-stylist. Harrell fills in many important biographical gaps. A welcome addition to what is becoming the HST cottage industry. Read it."

—Douglas Brinkley, editor of *The Proud Highway* and *Fear and Loathing in America*

"Memoir will likely please Hunter S. Thompson fans and appeal to readers with an interest in the beginnings of the post-modern era or the personal sacrifices involved in bringing serious written work to fruition."

—*Kirkus Indie Reviews*

"In the ever-expanding list of biographies and memoirs about Hunter S. Thompson, this latest offering, *Keep This Quiet!* by Margaret

A. Harrell, is quite simply a breath of fresh air. . . . What sets *Keep This Quiet!* apart is the extent to which Harrell explores the question of identity and myth, in her quest to simultaneously answer questions concerning her own character and that of one Hunter S. Thompson. As Harrell writes early on—"Who was he? There was no indication how complicated that answer was."

—Rory Patrick Feehan, PhD, owner of https://totallygonzo.org

"Three men, embodiments of three different dimensions of the late 1960's Zeitgeist—wispy dissolution, language-charged intellect, and Gonzo persona-building—are brought together by Harrell to invoke a world of passion and commitment . . . *Keep This Quiet!* is at once noisy, sensual, and word-drunk, as well as quietly intimate and full of Harrell's wonder at her luck. While most readers will come to this book for the Thompson content, in truth all the portraits here—all four of them—are compelling and often touching."

—W. C. Bamberger, *Rain Taxi Review*

"This is no ordinary book about or including Thompson. It's a memoir detailing personal relationships with three authors, the main focus being on Hunter. . . . [I] must stress that this book, as a memoir is quite deep and holds the door open for the reader. While Hunter is a huge selling point, the book has the legs to stand alone."

—Martin Flynn, owner of https://hstbooks.org

Representative Reviews—*Keep* THIS *Quiet Too!*–IV, rev. ed.

Keep THIS *Quiet Too! More Adventures with Hunter S. Thompson, Milton Klonsky, Jan Mensaert*

"A passionately written memoir that doesn't sit around being fit and proper and straight-laced. If I can use a well-worn phrase here, 'it lifts the lid on so many things.' . . . As a key to the lives of these three writers it is idiosyncratic and in age where blandness is the norm it is a pleasure to go on her journey and find out a little about what made these men tick and what drove her to them."

—*Beat Scene* (UK paper magazine)

Keep This Quiet! III: Initiations

"This is the third and highly recommended title in Margaret Harrell's outstanding *Keep This Quiet!* autobiographical series. A fascinating and very well written personal story, *Keep This Quiet! III: Initiations* is very highly recommended for both community and academic library collections. Also exceptionally commended are the first two volumes in this outstanding series, *Keep This Quiet! My Relationship with Hunter S. Thompson, Milton Klonsky, and Jan Mensaert,* and *Keep THIS Quiet Too!*"

—Midwest Book Review

Keep This Quiet! IV, rev ed: *Ancient Secrets Revealed*

"As though it arrived with a full legion of angelic messengers and masters of light, from the moment I touched this book, its energy began to flow through me. If you are ready to welcome energetic shifts toward enlightenment, this book is for you. This beautifully written volume of wisdom provides attunements as you meander through its pages joining Margaret on her journey."

—Diana Henderson, author of *Gathering of Angels* (*The Michael Saga*)

"Margaret Harrell's blending and merging the whole of a human being and beyond into the cosmos is astounding writing and what a lifetime Journey she has taken to arrive to this book. I feel Margaret is zipping around and catching the flavors of the world, the universe and Beyond. She is working with a whole new and different combined East-West and Middle Paradigm."

—Suzanne V. Brown, PhD, psychologist, former VP, Exceptional Human Experience Network

"Margaret Harrell is a skilled professional writer with excellent ability to communicate and weave esoteric ideas about science, psychology, philosophy, and spirituality. Richard Unger's channeled hand analysis description of her as a 'grand synthesizer' was apt and accurate."

—Ron Rattner, author of the Silly Sutras website and subject, actor in the film *Walks with Ron*, a spiritual memoir.

ABOUT THE AUTHOR

The author of the coffee table collectible *The* Hell's Angels *Letters* (Norfolk Press), the *Keep This Quiet!* I–IV memoir series, as well as *Particle Pinata Poems*, the artbook *Cloud Conversations*, and a host of others, Harrell copy-edited Hunter S. Thompson's first book, *Hell's Angels*. HST acknowledged her in *Gonzo Letters* 2. She is also a book editor, cloud photographer, and advanced meditation teacher in the LuminEssence school of light body and luminous body consciousness exploration, mentor to those wanting to maximize their potential.

Thank You for Reading My Book

Authors live by readers and their reviews. If you enjoyed *Space Encounters: III: Inserting Consciousness into Collisions, 2023,* I would deeply appreciate an honest positive review on Amazon and/or another platform. I will read every word you write and benefit from the comments.

Thank you again and God bless.